HEAD **STRONG**
A PARENTING SURVIVAL KIT
FOR REDUCING TENSION
AND BUILDING SELF-ESTEEM

HEAD **STRONG**
A PARENTING SURVIVAL KIT
FOR REDUCING TENSION
AND BUILDING SELF-ESTEEM

TED AYLLON, PH.D.

Performance Management Publications (PMP)

Performance Management Publications (PMP)
3344 Peachtree Road NE, Suite 1050
Atlanta, GA 30326
678.904.6140
www.PManagementPubs.com

ISBN-13: 978-0-937100-22-6

ISBN-10: 0-937100-22-6

2 3 4 5 6 7

Cover and text Design: James Omedo
Editor: Gail Snyder
Production Coordinator: Laura-Lee Glass

PMP books are available at special discounts for bulk purchases
by corporations, institutions, and other organizations.
For more information, please call 678.904.6140, ext. 131 or e-mail
info@aubreydaniels.com

To the parents and children who, over time, have helped me translate complex psychological, behavioral, and relational concepts into family interactions that result in parental trust and an increase in a child's personal responsibility.

ACKNOWLEDGMENTS

Initially, this book was written for an academic audience but over time it changed to a practical parent guide. This was largely through feedback from colleagues who read portions of this manuscript. I wish to thank Bob Sommer, Lou L'Abbate, Mike Milan, Helen Coale, and Mike Zeiler for their valuable comments and helpful encouragement. It was Aubrey Daniels who asked me if I had a book I wanted published who made it possible for me to finish it, and Darnell Lattal who encouraged me to view my work as potentially helpful in the general area of human relations. I wish to express my sincerest appreciation to both.

CONTENTS   ஃ HEAD **STRONG**

PREFACE

I taught at Georgia State University and practiced clinical behavioral psychology for 30 years. During my tenure as a university professor, I designed a variety of therapeutic studies involving children with difficult emotional and behavioral problems. These clinical studies were largely implemented by graduate students under my supervision. In close collaboration with parents, we examined the effectiveness of various parenting styles toward understanding and remediating a wide range of children's problems. The results from these studies were substantial, positive, and timely. These, and related findings, were soon corroborated by research clinicians and others. Novel to the approach was the notion that parents themselves could bring about the desired changes in their children if they were given hands-on training which translated into how to act and react to a child's challenging behaviors.

This strategy has special benefits. First, through special coaching, parents with a difficult child learn to act in alternative ways that reduce demanding and confrontational behavior and replace it with helpful, considerate, and respectful interactions. Second, this approach makes it possible for a child to acquire new behaviors and attitudes where they matter most – at home with the family. Third, in the case of especially difficult children, this approach supplements the impact of professional therapy. In short, this strategy empowers parents to act as the designated agents for behavioral and emotional change for their child.

FOREWORD

Problematic children confront parents with a variety of disruptive and unacceptable behaviors. Most of these involve disobedience and defiance, as well as irresponsible and socially inappropriate behaviors. The challenge for parents is how to deal with such behaviors in a timely manner. Many interactions with a difficult child are repetitive, revolve around the same issues, and leave parents emotionally debilitated, and often guilt-ridden. Today's parents need and deserve all the help they can get.

Techniques to arrest and transform problematic behaviors involve learning the why and the how of change. The tongue-in-cheek quip "if only they came with an instruction manual . . ." expresses every parent's frustration. This book is not necessarily that instruction manual. However, it shares a proven method that enables parents to engage difficult children in productive interactions that also reduce stress and frustration.

To understand problematic behavior we need to examine patterns of child-parent interaction and to focus on the reciprocal influence that child and parent have on one another. The parent-child interaction is a two-way street. In these interactions, the parent influences the child's behavior and the child influences the parents' behavior. Therefore, to understand how a child develops unwanted, unusual, and persistent behaviors, we need to look at the effect of what parents do in reaction to what a child says and does.

The strategic approach described here identifies the WHY or "purpose" of a child's misbehavior by examining what he gains or avoids in so behaving. Simply put, what does the problematic behavior do for him?

Problematic behavior can be understood in terms of a personal cost-benefit analysis to the child.

What does appropriate behavior COST a child?

To a difficult child, behaving appropriately takes too much work, too much time away from his fun and, in a word, it's too much trouble. To such a child, behaving appropriately is not worth the personal cost in effort, inconvenience, boredom, and frustration involved. Therefore, he is unlikely to listen to instructions and comply with typical parental expectations. To a difficult child there is a personal COST involved in behaving appropriately.

Over the last decade there has been a rise in the frequency and intensity of children's inappropriate behavior both at home and also in school. Learning to reduce those costly behavior patterns is not only good for parents but for the larger culture. It is not a casual or private family matter, but a critical issue to the health and well-being of us all.

How does inappropriate behavior BENEFIT a child?

For many children, behaving inappropriately often results in real personal benefits such as greater attention, concern, and even exemption from meeting minimal expectations. Indeed, many parents excuse a child from assuming basic responsibilities such as getting ready to catch the school bus in the morning, keeping up with homework, sleeping in his own bed, or even feeding the family's pet. Further, some parents will allow, tolerate, and accept problematic behaviors such as breaking things, being screamed at, or physically challenged, if they think it will help a child to express anger or to feel accepted. These circumstances help explain how a difficult child BENEFITS from misbehaving.

Contrary to the belief of many parents, problematic behavior is almost never symptomatic of some hidden cause. Rather the cause can be seen and understood quickly. The cause of such behavior patterns can be summarized as arising out of unintended consequences established by the parents in interacting with the child. What you see is a child's effort to adapt and deal with the prevailing social practices at home, often through what appears to be outrageous acts. Those actions are easily understood as the natural outcome of how behavior is shaped and maintained. It does not mean that the child is simply bad or willful or stubborn or any other label. Rather the pattern is one of parental and child interactions that maintain and often accelerate outrageous patterns that are predictable. They are maintained by consequences and they can be changed by consequences.

The home is where change can be first introduced and where a child can practice interpersonal and socially related skills such as coping with frustration and self-management. In the context of a loving and structured environment, parents help replace inappropriate behavior with appropriate behavior through an approach that increases home-based motivation and self-corrective consequences. Parents are in charge of a child's social development because they are the first and most influential agents of emotional and behavioral change. They have enormous capacity to create a center of calm certainty and predictive reactions that allow the child to feel safe and secure as he or she practices new and positive skills.

At the outset, we acknowledge that most parents want the best for their children. In general, parents act to protect a child from what they perceive are dangerous activities. Above all, parents want their children to be healthy and happy. Also, they want them to be respectful, responsible, and caring. However, sometimes, even parents' best efforts do not achieve the intended result. Specifically, in an effort to manage their child, parents often use practices that unintentionally encourage unwanted or unusual behaviors, and at a minimum, keep the unwanted behaviors alive.

Children tire parents by repeating the very thing they are told not to do. Paradoxically, parents also find themselves repeating the same commands and instructions that do not work. Each party is not listening to the other and they keep recycling the same interaction. To change the dynamics of this interaction one of the parties has to do something different. It is the parents' responsibility to discover how to change.

The methods described in this book rest on a well-researched fact: the emotional makeup and behavior of a child is largely influenced by the way in which parents interact with him/her on a day-to-day basis. The intent of this book is to equip parents with practices that have been found effective across a variety of difficult and challenging issues involving the relationship between a child and parent. Loving but exhausted parents will find specific guidelines to help a child choose to give up problematic behavior in a natural and positive way.

Head Strong presents and discusses a new parental approach that is both rooted in the natural real world as well as in the author's 30 years of research and practice working with children and their families. This book examines how the conditions that are likely to produce counterproductive and negative behaviors in a child may be replaced by alternative conditions that foster productive and positive behaviors.

This book also provides a road map to achieving a loving, interactional, effective approach to parenting. This goal is best achieved with the cooperation of parents or significant others who live with the child. A menu of solutions is included to drastically reduce unnecessary and counterproductive dependency and to develop a child's self-control, self-sufficiency, and self-esteem. Child and parent relations involve daily reactions that each comes to learn and expect from the other. These reactions are natural to both. Over time, some of these reactions come to define a child (Carly is really demanding" and "Vic's afraid of his own shadow." Also, some of these reactions come to define a parent as well ("Mom is such a worrier" and "Dad lets Angie get away with murder.") When this is the case, the reaction to each other keeps them repeating the same type of counterproductive and negative pattern.

Adjusting the parents' natural style of interaction for greater effectiveness is the key to unlocking positive behavioral and emotional changes in a difficult child.

The youth wondered what he
should be.

His prof said, "You're missing
the key.

"Life's not to be but to do.
Pick a task, follow through.

"You'll live ever after most
happily."

From Jack Oliver's Shakespeare Got It Wrong, It's Not "To Be," It's "To Do."
The Autobiographical Memoirs of a Lucky Geophysicist.
(Cornell University 1998)

CHAPTER ONE

A CHILD NEEDS LOVE, ATTENTION, AND PARENTAL CONNECTION

Parenting is not easy. Parenting difficult children is often a lot of work, and can be more emotionally draining and debilitating than anyone is willing to admit. Sometimes, a child behaves in a way that defies comprehension. Even when parents give a child much love, understanding, and emotional support, these efforts seem to make little or no difference. The child keeps repeating the same problematic, negative behavior, and over time exhausts his parents in their efforts to help him. Here you will read about such children and about an approach that empowers parents to talk and act in a way that induces a child to replace clinging, dependent, argumentative, and defiant behaviors with appropriate and positive behaviors.

As we embark on our journey we might start by asking a few questions:

Why is an academically good student barely able to get to school?

Doreen has a hard time waking up in the morning. She daydreams, seems to be in a fog in the morning, is poorly organized while getting ready, and misses the school bus while she is still getting dressed. That's Dreamy Doreen, a twelve-year-old.

Why has a boy quit speaking at home and communicates only through sign language?

Sammy is a nice, bright, and lovable child. In school he participates well and responds to direct questions. At home, however, he communicates his needs by pointing and gesturing. He will not talk. Sammy can speak but it seems that he does not want to "use his words." That's Silent Sammy, a five-year-old.

Why does a lively girl insist on sleeping every night with her parents?

Flora is a delightful, well-adjusted child who adores her parents, is doing well in school, and has many friends. Nobody would believe that such a wonderful and well-adjusted girl is terrified to sleep alone. She moans, cries, and begs to sleep with her parents and has done so for the last four years. That's Fearful Flora, a nine-year-old.

Why does a healthy boy get so sick in the morning that he cannot go to school?

Simon is a sensitive child from a loving family. Sometimes he suffers from stomach pains that make him scream and cry so much that he has to stay at home and miss school. Mom does everything she can to make sure her son is in good health and is not simply exaggerating his condition. Still, seeing her son crying and doubled up in pain convinces her to seek help. That's Sickly Simon, a seven-year-old.

How can a girl be popular in school, but a "monster" at home?

Annie is bright, cute, and well liked by her schoolteachers. Yet, at home, she argues about everything and resists complying with her parents' requests. Her parents are loving and sensitive and they do not want to suppress her "spunky" quality. That's Annie, a seven-year-old.

There are many such examples, but by now you get the picture.

What is wrong with these kids?

These children, and others like them, seldom show any serious physical or psychological pathology to account for their problematic behavior. In general, these children have average or above-average intelligence. They are not lost souls. These children have grown up in a highly stimulating electronic environment programmed to maintain a child's interest through a complex mix of games, music, and quasi-social feedback. These children enjoy electronic entertainment and respond appropriately to the rapid pace of exciting audiovisual stimuli presented through various electronic devices. The rest of their time at home, however, these children are not focused, are easily distracted, do not listen, and do not do what they are asked. While operating various electronic devices, these children are focused and attentive for long periods of time, so much so that they hardly stop to socialize, rest, or eat. It is estimated that these children are "plugged in" for more than 50 hours a week.

However, there is a contrast between attentiveness while interacting with a computer game and attentiveness in class. Admittedly, a teacher cannot easily present the teaching material with the same high-interest value of video games and other electronic entertainment in terms of color, sound, and motion; nor can she do it at the speed of such devices. These conditions alone may limit a teacher's impact and result in inattentive, unfocused, and easily distracted and bored students. Some students are even resistant to most efforts to teach them. One might characterize these children as difficult, problematic, spoiled, or high maintenance.

Why does a child persist in not listening to parents and instead relies on them to get him out of trouble?

Here is a quick and working answer: a child behaves in problematic and sometimes dramatic ways because this often shifts the family's attention and concern to him. These are parents who care. They love and want their children to grow into happy individuals who cooperate, are considerate of others, and behave responsibly. These parents have done everything they know to help, but their child continues to repeat very problematic behaviors.

Why does a child keep repeating the same negative behavior when he knows it is going to get him into trouble?

Recurrent misbehavior occurs largely because the parental

style of dealing with it often locks child and parent in a negative feedback loop they cannot easily break. The cases described previously include cycles of blame, placating, and avoidance. The whole process leaves parents and child exhausted, disappointed, hurt, and often angry at one another.

What do parents do to change a child's misbehavior?

Ordinarily, parents try either to ignore or dismiss misbehavior, but when pushed, parents will give a child a harsh tongue lashing. Other times, they send a child to time-out which means banishing the child to his room or to some other area in the house for a brief period of time. Some parents use this period to sit with the child, asking for him to explain his actions, to see the error of his ways, and to apologize. Other parents use this period to strengthen their emotional bond and to remind a child how much they love him and to discuss how his actions hurt his family. This is a time when parents provide soothing words and reassurance to calm a distraught child. As a child continues to misbehave despite all efforts, parents start to take things away from him such as access to TV, computer games, the Internet, cell phone, and the like. When parents reach their limit of tolerance of misbehavior they ground the child. During this period, a child is not allowed to play outside; nor is he allowed to accept friends' invitations to go out, attend a movie, or a concert. These privileges are unavailable to him for whatever length of time parents decide. This could be for a short period (such as a few days) or as long as a month or more. Some parents may send a child to bed without dessert while others may resort to spanking a child for unacceptable behavior.

Although these parental efforts are somewhat different from one another, they all are aimed at stopping a child's misbehavior. Generally speaking, these efforts work with some children. However, a collateral effect of such efforts is that they often produce in a child conflicting feelings of approach and avoidance to his parents. He may still love his parents but he also mistrusts them.

What makes a child misbehave?

Research data shows time and time again evidence for three major behavioral findings:

1. A child seeks the parents' love, acceptance, and approval. A child's basic motivation is social.

2. Misbehavior is developed by a child's immediate social environment and emerges largely within the context of daily social interaction with parents.

> **Takeaway #1**
>
> **Everything a child does involves an integration of feelings, thoughts, and actions—all largely learned first in interaction with parents.**

3. The linkage between a child's behavior and a parent's reaction to it is a critical factor in understanding the rise and fall of misbehavior.

Related data show that a child's complex behavior develops rapidly in an interactive social environment. Indeed, as a child spends time at home with his family, he learns social values, expectations, and family traditions that are passed on from parents to children in their day-to-day interactions. By watching his parents' behavior, he learns to interact socially and emotionally.

Problematic children are often made not born.

Many parents have been persuaded that a child will grow into a responsible young adult if given a good deal of freedom to express himself and make his own decisions. Accordingly, parents give a child a variety of choices: what to wear to pre-school, what to eat, where and when to eat, where and when to go to bed, and how to address his mom and dad. At home, these children do what they please. They grow up with little or no limits. They leave their coats, shoes, books, soft drinks, and food, all over the house, and they become upset and even abusive toward parents when they are asked to clean up. Further, they blame parents or siblings when they cannot find their "stuff." Some children even threaten to call or inform the Department of Family and Children Services (DFACS) if a parent decides to use punishment. Emphasis is on the self and even on resisting influence by others. As their attention and concern is for the self they are often unaware and even neglectful of the effect of their actions on their parents. Their behavior in the community also has no social limits. For example, an eight-year-old boy went to a restroom and when he found it locked he proceeded to kick it until the man inside opened it. When the man told him that this was no way to treat private property, the child ignored him completely and slammed the door on him. When the man found the child's parents, he described the incident to them, but they minimized their son's actions by saying, "He doesn't really mean it . . . he is just upset . . . he's not really like that."

The main point here is that a child from early on is encouraged to make his own choices. At times, some of these choices are good. At other times, they are not so good. Even then, a child's own experience teaches him to expect his parents to pick up the "pieces" from his bad choices and shield him from the consequences of his own actions. Not surprisingly, he learns that making bad choices is not something to worry about.

Overprotecting a difficult child has unintended consequences.

Loving parents are naturally protective of their child, and this is to the good. However, excusing a child for his repetitive, offensive conduct has three unintended consequences:

1. It spares a child the experience of feeling the consequences of his own actions.

2. It gives a child "permission" to spend little or no effort on his own behalf.

3. It prevents him from learning how to cope with even mild frustrations.

These unintended consequences train a child to count on being rescued from suffering the consequences of his own actions. Also, they undermine individual initiative and weaken personal responsibility. A child becomes a good "reader" of his parents' likely reactions to his misbehavior. As he learns which parent is the "softie" and which is the "enforcer" he manipulates them to his advantage. Following is such an example.

Dreamy Doreen, a twelve-year-old

Doreen is typically late to catch the school bus and Mom has to rush and drive her to school. To make sure Doreen got enough sleep, Mom had Doreen go to bed by nine o'clock during the school week. Still, Doreen had a hard time waking up in the morning, so Mom had to help her get dressed and get something to eat so that she could be on time. When Dad told Doreen that it was time for her to grow up and act her age she became very upset, cried, told him she did not want to talk to him any more, and to leave her alone. Since Dad's job took him away from home nearly every week, he felt he had no choice except to leave Mom to take care of the problem. Despite all Mom's efforts, Doreen seemed to be daydreaming much of the time and unable to get organized in time to catch the school bus. Mom did not want Doreen to be late for school because it might get her in trouble with the teacher. Mom knew that Doreen was a good student, and worried that being late to school might reflect poorly on her academic accomplishments. It seemed that Mom was more worried about her daughter being late for school than Doreen herself. When Doreen missed the school bus, Mom had to drive her to school while complaining about Doreen's irresponsible behavior and getting into an argument with her. Mom felt harassed and terribly conflicted because after dropping Doreen off at school she had to hurry back home and get herself ready to go to work. She wondered why a smart girl like Doreen could not understand how important it was to be ready in time to catch the school bus.

What was done to help Doreen learn to accept responsibility for herself?

As Doreen was not accepting responsibility for getting ready in the morning and taking the bus to school, Mom had gradually become Doreen's personal assistant and lady-in-waiting. Mom was in charge of waking her up, dressing, and prodding her to hurry as Doreen sat down, or walked dreamily in a kind of reverie instead of getting ready to eat the breakfast that Mom had prepared for her. Typically, Doreen was too slow to catch the school bus so she missed it and Mom had to drive her to school while Doreen ate breakfast in the car. Doreen did not fret or act anxious when she missed the school bus. She was not worried about it. Instead, she seemed to be quite comfortable letting Mom do the worrying and driving.

After determining what the situation was at home, a morning routine was designed after consulting with Mom. Mom agreed to try an alternative way to help Doreen become responsible for arriving to school on time. She was coached to allow Doreen to experience arriving late to school. One morning, Mom woke Doreen as usual, and then prodded her to get dressed before she went to the kitchen to fix breakfast. When she came back to Doreen's room, Doreen was still daydreaming and slowly getting dressed while watching TV. Mom calmly helped her but now she did not nag or rush her. Doreen was, as usual, very slow and by the time she came down for breakfast, she had not only missed the school bus, but she could not get to school on time even if Mom drove her there. Still, Mom did not act worried nor did she scold or berate her daughter for being late.

On the way to school Doreen suddenly became terribly worried, anxious, and even frantic. She was going to really be late and worried about what her teacher would say to her. As she became conscious of the fact that she was already late for school, she started blaming Mom for not getting her ready on time. Mom did not argue with her daughter and instead concentrated on driving the car. As they arrived late for school, Mom let Doreen off and left immediately to avoid being late to work herself.

When Doreen returned from school that day, she was very upset. She told Mom that the teacher told her in no uncertain terms that she expected students to be on time. Doreen felt terrible that she had disappointed her teacher by being late. That evening Doreen set her own alarm clock. The next morning, Doreen woke up on her own, got dressed, and when Mom called her for breakfast, came down, didn't turn the TV on, ate her breakfast, and left to catch the school bus with time to spare! From that day on, Doreen chose to get herself up on her own and ready in time to catch the school bus. Mom was surprised and delighted that her daughter had finally become a responsible kid.

It seems that Mom and daughter shared the same concern about being late to school. Yet, as long as Mom shielded Doreen from the natural consequences of being late for school, there was no basis for her daughter to fret and get anxious. Once Mom allowed Doreen to make direct contact with the natural consequences of being late to school, Doreen quickly mended her ways. She assumed responsibility for getting up in the morning, getting dressed, and catching the school bus on time.

Silent Sammy, a five-year-old

Sammy's parents' major concern was that one day he quit speaking at home. His parents did whatever was needed to help him speak, including prompting the words and having him repeat words. Still, despite their loving efforts, he just did not use his words.

> **Takeaway #2**
>
> The more parents "filter" out everyday inconveniences, the more a child relies on parental help.

He knew how to speak, but he just did not seem to want to speak.

Behavior of this sort is often clinically described as "selective mutism." This is a psychological condition in which a child may speak in some settings, such as at home, but may not do so in others, such as in school. Here, the situation was reversed: Sammy communicated verbally rather well in kindergarten. At home, however, he communicated his needs by pointing and using sign language. When he wanted something to eat, he did not ask for the food item. Instead, he pointed to the item. That seemed to work for him because Mom knew Sammy well and anticipated what he wanted. He did the same with other items like clothes. He pointed to the closet and Mom ordinarily picked the items she knew he wanted. The same thing happened with toys and other items. Clearly, Mom became Sammy's personal valet who got what Sammy pointed to. Still, occasionally, Mom misunderstood what it was he pointed to, and when that happened he became emotionally distraught and moaned and

> **Takeaway #3**
>
> A child learns to rely on parents, and significant others, to rescue him from self-produced discomfort and annoyance.

screamed in disgust until Mom self-corrected rather quickly. Sammy's selective muteness suggests that, accidentally, he discovered that this attention-getting behavior resulted in love, soothing, comfort, in the form of direct personal assistance provided by his parents. In a sense, he learned to behave as if he did not know how to speak. That is why his parents acted at times as speech coaches and at other times as teachers of a deaf-mute child, sometimes combining persuasion and rewards, and sometimes taking things away from him. All these efforts led to no discernable change in his mute-like behavior at home. Instead, he seemed to grow comfortable with his parents' help rather than motivated to use his words. After a while his parents got tired of this pointing routine. More importantly, they worried and wondered what would happen to Sammy if he grew up totally dependent on them to manage his daily life.

What was done to help Silent Sammy resume talking to his parents?

As Sammy was not using his words as expected, his parents agreed to try another approach to help their child. They were coached to become less efficient in the timing and delivery of the items that Sammy pointed to. The idea was to allow him to learn to be patient by waiting a few minutes before Mom or Dad "divined" what he wanted. His parents were no longer 100 percent but only 50 percent efficient in their point-reading routine. This meant that if Sammy pointed to potatoes, Mom gave him the food item next to it, say, green beans. When he pointed to the clothes in his closet, such as a pair of jeans, Mom would get a different item that was next to it, such as a T-shirt. Acting as if she had helped him, she moved on to busy herself with some other task. When he moaned and complained, Mom excused herself, and said something like, "Sorry Sweetie; let me finish what I'm doing, and I'll be there in a minute, OK?" At other times, when he pointed to an item, his parents hesitated as if they were not sure what he wanted. They looked puzzled and took a minute or so to "understand" what he wanted.

The goal was to continue to help Sammy in a loving, but also inefficient way, to get what he wanted. His parents were to convey to him the sense that they were doing the best they could to help but that their best was, unfortunately, not good enough.

Initially, Sammy reacted to the new approach by moaning and becoming irritated at the mistakes his parents made in interpreting what he wanted. A few times he actually threw

Tip #1	**To discourage unwanted behavior, allow the natural inconveniences to flow from unwanted behavior.**

a tantrum when Mom mistook his pointing. Finally, he could no longer contain himself and screamed at his mom, "That's wrong! That's not what I want!" In a few days he spoke without the critical remarks and found that his parents understood his words better than his pointing. Within a week's time Sammy chose to express himself verbally in a loud and clear voice: "Milk, please!" "I would like more macaroni." "I want my jeans." "Where's my blue T-shirt?" His parents reported that Sammy was gradually talking more and that when he tried to point to items, a reminder of, "I'm not sure what you want; please use your words," seemed sufficient to get him to express his needs verbally. As Sammy increased his verbal expression, the natural (and positive) consequence was that his parents spent more fun time with him playing board games and reading stories to him.

Following are a few principles for parents to remember:

1. From very early on, a child explores his surroundings and soon discovers that interacting with parents is comforting, stimulating, and fun.

2. Parents give a child love, attention, and related personal benefits when he behaves well, but also (unintentionally) when he behaves badly.

3. Parents tend to overlook the emergence of a child's problematic behavior.

4. A child needs a home-based structure within which he feels safe to practice a variety of skills to develop confidence in himself.

5. Helplessness is learned and can be unlearned.

6. Behaving responsibly is learned, as is behaving irresponsibly.

7. Parents are largely responsible for managing consequences to improve socially appropriate behavior.

Let's go back to the original question as to what parents can do to change a child's misbehavior. The short answer is "plenty."

Do you recognize your parenting style?

Think about how you respond to your child's demands. Think about how you respond when your child ignores your request or constantly "forgets" to complete the task expected of him. Do you find yourself doing his task to end the hassle? Think about how you respond when a dramatic episode occurs. Do you find yourself giving in just for a moment of peace?

Before you commit to changing a child's behavior, it will help you to review the role you, the parent, play when dealing with misbehavior. To this end, check the I-statements that best describe the way you deal with repeated misbehavior.

1. I act as the peacemaker and tend to minimize misbehavior.

2. I tend to overlook misbehavior, and find "good" reasons to explain it.

3. I tend to shield a child from the consequences of his misbehavior.

4. I give a child the benefit of the doubt as to what really happened.

5. I tend to placate and give in when a child promises to stop misbehaving.

6. I try to compensate for my spouse's style of dealing with a child.

7. I just worry and tend to be a self-blamer.

8. I tend to go from being a disciplinarian to being a softie.

Do not feel bad if you checked one or more of these statements. These descriptions characterize what loving and well-meaning parents often do to deal with a difficult child. Besides, these reactions often help avoid highly charged emotional scenes involving you and your child. They work, even if only for a time. That's why you are likely to react the way you do. In effect, you gain a temporary sense of control and a respite from feeling frustrated and generally upset. Admittedly, these very actions also enable a child to continue reacting in unfeeling and irresponsible ways. Still, you wonder, Why is it so hard for him to understand that all you are trying to do is to help him?

Understand a child's emotions and behavior.

Parents need to gain perspective to understand and appreciate that a difficult child is not necessarily mean, stupid, lazy, or crazy! We need to understand a child's emotions and behavior to be more effective in our efforts to help him change. There are many different views on how to do so.

Focus on feelings.

One view focuses on asking a child to look inward to find out why he does what he does. For example, using this approach, we would ask Doreen to get in touch with her feelings because we think it is her feelings that cause her to behave the way she does. This is a good start for us to get clues as to what Doreen is experiencing and feeling. But this approach quickly runs us into trouble. She seems to day dream a lot and is not reflective or articulate about her own feelings. To further complicate things, Doreen is likely to express only what is safe or acceptable to her parents. In short, she is likely to tell them only what they want to hear.

Focus on actions.

Another view is that we need to focus on a child's behavior. For example, Doreen was often late to catch the school bus, which made everyone wonder what was wrong with her. Still, by focusing on her being late to catch the bus, we are dealing with facts. However, this information is incomplete. She and her mother agreed that they had frequent quarrels on school days, but Doreen does not necessarily acknowledge her role in these arguments. As far as she is concerned, quarrels happen. She does not seem to give much thought to them. What Doreen knows is that she gets to school on time. So we are back to the initial problem.

Focus on feelings and actions.

We need to extend the information from both views and ask, "Where and when does a child misbehave?" Answers to this line of questioning would provide us with information regarding the impact of misbehavior on her primary social environment. What was the impact on Doreen's parents when she was late to catch the school bus? What was their reaction? What exactly did they do about it? What was the impact on Doreen? Answers to these questions will give us clues as to the source of motivation for Doreen's actions. For example, a child may behave in a submissive way when Dad is around but be demanding and difficult when he is away at work. A child may be particularly difficult when he is asked to do his homework or help with chores but be relatively undemanding when he is left to his own activities.

So we need to realize that the focus on feelings or on behavior alone does not give us sufficient information to know how to help a child . However, if we regard these two views as complementary rather than in competition, then the choice is not whether to focus on feelings or on actions. Instead, we factor in the relevant conditions in a child's immediate environment that influence his feelings, thinking, and behavior.

A child's behavior is entwined with the social context that surrounds him. A child is most likely to misbehave when he is not feeling good about himself. When this is occurring at home, we want to know what is going on there. It may be that he thinks everyone is too busy or too distant to stop and listen to him. Similarly, when he misbehaves in school, we want to know what is going on with his interactions there. For example, Chris complains daily about the amount of homework he has to do because he hardly has enough time to play war games on the computer.

Mom is very worried about her daughter Alexa who is shy and complains she does not have friends and that nobody likes her. Lately, Mom has noticed that Alexa filches money from Mom's purse and "lends" it to kids she would like to have as friends.

Both children's behaviors (thinking, feeling, doing) can be better understood if we do not separate behavior from the social environment in which it takes place. Awareness of a child's immediate social world gives us clues as to the meaning of misbehavior. This is the general context for the approach followed in this book.

> **Takeaway #4**
>
> **The meaning of a child's behavior is socially nested at home, school, or with his peers.**

A child needs love, attention, and parental connection.

A child is a social being. The major source of motivation for a child is social. A child enjoys being the focus of attention. A child thrives in a positive social environment. Along with finding out how things work in his immediate physical environment, he also learns how his social world works. Initially, he does so first by producing sounds, and later, a combination of sounds and gestures, and finally through words. All along, a child is seeking attention and a social connection. His verbal skills gradually develop in interaction with family members as he reacts or responds to his parents' efforts to promote communication. Research on early child development indicates that parents who interact verbally with their young children, and pay attention to their language experience increase the child's learning tools to effectively interact with complex tasks in school. A child's language repertoire is further established by his parents' feedback and responsiveness. These conditions make it more likely for a child to learn how to express his needs or wants in a way that his parents and significant others appear delighted to attend to and to convey the love and warmth they have for him. The overall impact of good experiences on a child is that he will feel motivated, confident, and comfortable in seeking similar interactions in the future.

To become a likeable, competent, and socially responsive child requires frequent, loving, and positive social practice with people, starting with his parents. It is through such social practice that he learns from others, not just how to behave, but what to like, what activities to explore and practice, and even how to think and feel. In a word, a child's behavior (emotions and thought) and that of his parents are fundamentally intertwined, interactive, and nested in a social environment.

CHAPTER TWO

THE CHILD IS NOT OUR ONLY CONCERN

Change begins with you, the parent. Yes, parents are the key to changing a child's way of behaving. That's right. A child cannot change by himself. This perspective turns the conventional approach upside down. The focus is not just on the difficulties of the child. Rather, it also emphasizes the parents' own difficulties in dealing with him.

Parents are not perfect. For that matter, children are not either. The issue is not about perfection when raising children. Rather, the issue for parents is to do the best they can. That is as much as anyone can do. Parents can be proud for all the loving things they do for their children. If their efforts do not always succeed, it's not for lack of trying on their part. In fact, most of the problems that parents are confronted with are by-products of the way they try to correct or solve the problem. In effect, the way they react to a problematic child becomes part of the very problem they are trying to deal with. Now, why is that? The answer is not a simple one.

Today, parents are often rushed at work, and, as soon as they arrive home, are also expected to meet the myriad demands of uncooperative, uncommunicative, passive-aggressive children at home. Sometimes, to cope with the kids' misbehavior at home, stressed-out parents tend to do what their own parents did with them. At other times, they tend to do the opposite: if their parents were structured and disciplined, they will try giving a child freedom and choices of what they eat, what they wear, and so on. The parents view these efforts as an improvement on their own parents' style of child rearing. Either way, when things are not working, both child and parent often become stuck, repeating the same ineffective interaction that makes each feel that it is impossible to live together under the same roof! In time, this interaction feels even choreographed as they cannot help repeating the same cycle of negative and unpleasant interaction with one another.

Sometimes, parents wonder why a child who seems so likeable and well behaved in school is so disrespectful and willful at home. Other times, parents experience the opposite situation: a child is well behaved and cooperative at home but disobedient and overly playful in school! Where is the real child in all of this? While parents may take solace in thinking that the "inner" child is really sweet and loving, others will judge him on his actions. Still, a child is often oblivious of the effect of his behavior on others (parents, teachers, and neighbors).

Naturally, parents want to know what is wrong with such a child. Basically, what's the meaning of his/her behavior? Early on s/he may be thought of as being a scaredy-cat, a mama's boy, lazy bones, forgetful, selfish, and even a mean child. Over time, s/he may be evaluated as having a special condition such as Separation Anxiety, Attention Deficit Disorder, Oppositional Disorder, and so on. Sometimes, these labels are helpful in that they point to certain observable characteristics displayed by a problematic child. More often, labels imply that a problematic child is a carrier of negative behavior and, therefore, not susceptible to change via changing parental practices at home.

To understand what may be going on with a problematic child, it is useful to review some of the features that may characterize your own style of child management. Consider your answers to the following questions:

1. Do you have some established structure or rule that allows a child to know when to go play, when to do homework, when to go to bed, and when to share time with parents?

2. Do you rely on criticism, punishment, and time-out to assure compliance?

3. Do you have physical closeness or distance between you and your child?

4. Do both parents agree that something needs to be done about the child's challenging behavior(s)?

5. Do you find that you are just too tired and have little energy and no time left to go around being positive when you are up to your ears just stopping your kids' usual sibling struggles and demanding

that they quit their computer games and related electronic "toys"?

Parents are in charge of socializing a child.

You may now be ready to acknowledge the powerful impact you have on your child by examining the following influences:

1. Your role in the development and maintenance of a child's appropriate as well as inappropriate behavior

2. Your home as the place where problematic behaviors emerge, develop, and where they are strengthened or weakened

3. Your focus on giving a child toys and access to computer games, iPods, Internet, cell phones, and other electronic devices to placate or lessen troublesome, disrespectful, and irresponsible behavior (Parents are now entering a post-excess period; finally understanding that reliance on material goods is not the answer to building a relationship with a child.)

4. Your emotional support to nurture and sustain enduring change in a child's social and academic gains.

LEARNING STYLES OF SOCIAL INTERACTION

Parents provide moral teachings and patterns of proper behavior for long-term social effectiveness. Social interpersonal relations are not static; they are in a constant process of change in response to changes in the social environment. This need not be a cause for confusion or discouragement.

Styles of social interaction are acquired through the subtle child-parent interaction at home. Learning interpersonal social skills is a very important goal in the socialization of a child. Historically, different cultures have socialized their children differently. The freedom and spontaneity that is often associated with American children, for example, is often viewed by other societies as reflecting irresponsible behavior, and, at a minimum, bad manners. Manners, a sense of propriety, saving face, embarrassment, or feeling guilty are largely the by-products of certain cultural practices in different social environments.

Today in America, defiant, confrontational, "in your-face" interactions may be viewed as styles of conduct that often benefit a child either in terms of getting his way or becoming the focus of attention of adults or peers. These ways of interacting owe their maintenance largely to parental styles of child management (or lack thereof).

Mindy, a smart and cute, brown-eyed, six-year-old, has been known to make a scene and to become the focus of attention particularly when people come to visit. At such times, Mindy bosses her mom around. When she calls her mom, she wants her "Right now!" As Mom tries to soothe her and persuade her that she's busy and that she'll only be gone for just a few minutes, Mindy screams: "You come back here right now, you hear? What do you think you're doing?" Sometimes, to avoid an ugly scene, Mom excuses herself for a few minutes and makes a deal with Mindy. She tells her she'll take her to McDonald's. But first, she has to promise that she'll quit hassling her. The child is now more reassured and answers, "OK, Mommy, I promise." Mom is actually rewarding Mindy's bossy behavior and empty promises to control herself. Sure enough, a short while later, Mindy repeats the very bossy pattern of behavior that has "worked" for her in the past. The pattern is already set: whenever Mindy misbehaves, Mom tries to correct her at first, but, once Mindy promises not to do it again Mom takes her to McDonald's to seal the "agreement."

Ruby Anne, a nine-year-old, constantly argues with and contradicts her parents and is uncooperative and even defiant. It does not take too much for her to become impatient and demanding. For example, when her mother asks if she would read a page from her school book, Ruby Anne tells her mom that she would rather watch cartoons. After a while, when Mom reminds her that it is time to do her homework, she refuses, adding "I don't want to do that. I'm having fun here!"(watching TV).

When it is bedtime, Mom asks Ruby Anne to go get ready, but Ruby Anne ignores Mom, and acts as though she has not heard her speak. When her mother, after many reminders, tells her that it's past her bedtime and attempts to guide her to the bedroom, Ruby Anne refuses to move, and screams, "I don't want to go. You can't make me!" flailing her arms and making it difficult for Mom to avoid getting hit. Mother tries to reason with her but to no avail. Dad is tired of this nightly routine and leaves it to Mom to deal with the situation. Finally, Mom gives in and tells her daughter that she can stay up, but only "for 10 more minutes!"

These two cases illustrate the fact that many children have learned that parents and significant others accept their misbehavior as something that just happens. These cases also illustrate the helplessness and sense of discomfort and stress experienced by parents when they have to deal with problematic behavior.

> **Takeaway #5**
>
> Placating a child when s/he misbehaves encourages more misbehavior.

Stress affects the whole family.

Parents are likely to encounter stress at work. This is particularly the case for working parents whose job is too demanding or not fulfilling. Added to this, when parents come home, they do not stop working. They prepare meals, do household chores, cleaning, laundry, and so on. They also go over a child's homework, get him ready to take a bath and to go to bed. As if that were not enough, coming home to kids who are uncooperative and even confrontational places additional stress on parents. Not surprisingly, under these conditions, a home becomes a kind of battleground where parents and children are caught in an emotional no-win situation involving bickering, quarreling, and tiresome confrontations.

Children may show a lack of self-control and respect for parents even in public places for all to see. Such children often have fun running around, yelling, climbing on tables, screaming, while blissfully unaware of their effect on others. Some public places find it difficult to maintain order. Recently the owner of a coffee shop in Chicago got tired of all the yelling and screaming and posted a sign requesting that children use their "indoor voices" when entering the shop. This did not go over well with many of the neighborhood mothers who considered boycotting the coffee shop. They felt it was unrealistic to expect children to control their voices and behave well, and they viewed the request as an insult to parents who were already doing their best under stressful conditions.

At the outset, then, we need to focus on the parental influence in the development of a child's mind and behavior. Specifically, we must look at our natural reaction and response to a child's problematic actions, including disrespectful and irresponsible behavior, and how these reactions tend to keep troublesome behavior alive and well.

Patrick, a thirteen-year-old, became very upset with Mom at the mall when he did not get his way. He continued to misbehave and was very disrespectful while riding home. When they got home, Mom asked Patrick to help her put things away, but he refused and went to play on the computer. When his friend came over to ask Patrick to play, Mom told her son that he could not leave the house because of his ugly behavior at the mall. However, after a lot of arguing, screaming, and promising he would do better next time, Mom let Patrick go play with his friend. Later that evening, while discussing the day with her husband, Mom wondered why Patrick seemed insensitive to the consequences of his behavior.

WHEN "CONSEQUENCES" DO NOT WORK

Patrick's mom typifies a misconception about consequences. A child may gradually learn to act with little concern for the consequences that follow his actions when the "consequences" are largely speeches and admonitions from parents. In Patrick's case Mom's initial reaction to his misbehavior was to not allow him to leave home. That was a good move on her part. However, Mom reversed herself and allowed him to go with his friend when Patrick promised to do better next time. By doing so, Mom is encouraging Patrick to simply promise to behave when he is in trouble. This means that Patrick will again misbehave when he does not get his way but will continue to promise to behave better to get what he wants and to avoid or reduce any penalty. In this case, Mom's consequences did work—in Patrick's favor.

Parental inconsistency encourages inconsistent behavior.

Often, parents are inconsistent in providing consequences for a child's problematic behavior. This means that periodically a child's inconsistent behavior will lead to parental attention or other concrete consequences that favor him. When this is the case, a child will be more likely to repeat the conflicting behavior so as to maximize positive outcomes and minimize negative ones.

For example, an eight-year-old boy is made fun of and teased by one of his classmates in school. His mother commiserates with him and tells him to just ignore his classmate. Father criticizes the boy as a "wimp" and directs him to defend himself physically. The child is conflicted as to what is the right thing to do. He does not know how to behave when he is teased in school. Now, he complains that he does not like school, or he simply withdraws to his room where he spends most of his time.

> **Takeaway #6**
>
> **A child is more likely to experience stress and act inconsistently when parents do not agree on setting limits and boundaries.**

When parents disagree on the standards of conduct, there will be an inconsistent application of consequences that will have the net effect of developing inconsistent behavior on the part of a child. An additional issue for a child is that he is most likely to believe that he is being asked to override his feelings of loyalty to one parent at the expense of disloyalty to the other. In such cases, no matter what a child's decision is, he will offend at least one of his parents. Under these circumstances, it is not surprising for a child to blow hot or cold and act inconsistently in his emotional reaction to either parent. Sometimes, parents complain that a child is difficult to be with, that he is unpredictable, that "you never know with him." When parents provide contrary or opposite reactions for the same behavior, they produce a child's conflicted behavior involving confusion in his feeling and thinking.

Keeper of the secret, Chrissy, a fifteen-year-old

Chrissy's parents believe that a child should be truthful with both of them. From time to time, however, her mother said to Chrissy, "Don't tell Dad that you saw that boy again because he'll get upset." This interaction with her mother creates a conflict which makes Chrissy uncomfortable and

rather anxious when her father wants to know about her social life. She feels horrible about lying to him, and tries to
be maniacally busy when she is around him. She loves her
father and wishes she could confide in him, but she feels
that she would betray her mother and possibly upset her father, causing trouble for herself.

Conflicting child's actions, feelings, and thoughts often reflect conflicting feedback from the child's parents ("Do
what I say, not what I do"). To bring about change, parents
need to shift their focus from the child to themselves. If
anything, a parent's customary reaction to misbehavior
often enables the child to repeat the same counterproductive
behavior over and over again. The net result of this process
keeps both child and parent stuck in a mutually negative
cycle of interaction.

PITTING ONE PARENT AGAINST THE OTHER

A child is likely to pit one parent against the other if their
reaction to doing so favors her. For example, Bernie, a
twelve-year-old girl, remembered always at the last minute
that she needed special paper, or pens, or some other item
that she just had to have for the next day of classes. Ordinarily, she mentioned this matter just when the family was
relaxing or busy with their own concerns. After a few times
of frantic runs to the store for one thing or another, her father started to balk and tell Bernie that she had to become
more responsible for her own work and that he would not
help her anymore. Bernie then pleaded with her mother,
who felt that it was not right to refuse to help her daughter,
so she did. This typically led to arguments between Mother

and Father as to the appropriate way to teach their daughter to be responsible. Mother felt that it was too much to expect Bernie to remember everything, while Dad felt it was time for Bernie to take responsibility for her schoolwork. One of the side-effects of such disagreements between parents is that the child's style of interaction is likely to persist because, unwittingly, one parent functions as the rescuer or "guardian angel."

> **Takeaway #7**
>
> **Conflicting and inconsistent parenting practices encourage inconsistent and contradictory behavior.**

Parents are often in conflict and in a state of denial.

Generally speaking, problematic children are neither neurologically impaired, nor suffering from some unknown learning disability. Even when they are engaged in fun activities, such as sports, some of these children will also argue with the coach, refuse to follow instructions, and become surly and defiant when admonished. There seems to be a growing trend for such children to act in impulsive and rowdy ways.

Parents often argue regarding the best way to deal with a child's problematic behavior. Sometimes, parents attribute a child's challenging behaviors to lack of attention, mood changes, or simply forgetfulness. At other times, they view misconduct and disobedience as just a phase or a stage the child is going through. Still, parents are made to feel inadequate and overwhelmingly guilty when dealing with their own difficult child. Admittedly, they love their child and will do anything to make him happy, including overlooking his problematic behavior and making all kinds of excuses and accommodations for inappropriate behavior in hopes that it will go away. For low-level misbehavior, this may be a good tactic. For high-level problematic behavior, however, accepting a child's misbehavior is converted into approval of such behavior. The net outcome of this process is that it makes it more likely for a child to repeat the pattern of misbehavior.

As the tension and pressure continue over time, parents tend to cope with a child's misbehavior through means of denial. At such times, parents may find temporary relief by putting in more time at work, going out with friends after work, and generally, delaying coming home.

Parents gradually adapt to misbehavior.

The incremental acceptance of disobedience often increases the frequency and intensity of the very behaviors parents are trying to change. Finally, to keep the peace within a household, parents acquiesce or end up doing the task they have repeatedly asked the child to do, such as cleaning their room or helping with the household chores. In the absence of an effective alternative, parents gradually adapt to and accept daily misbehavior as this is the only way they can survive.

Lila is a charming, bright, and full of energy six-year-old. She's a good student and her teachers love to have her in their class. At home, she shows her charming personality but she also shows a very strong stubborn and dramatic side. She cannot play a board game with Mom and her sister who is three years older without causing an emotional scene. When they try to correct her, she will break into crying and sometimes throws herself to the floor all the while blaming her sister for some imagined hurt. Much parental effort goes into soothing, reasoning, and pointing out to her that her sissy did not look, touch, or say anything against her and that she simply was much too touchy and ready for a quarrel when there was no need for that. Still, Lila basically ruins the moment for the rest of the family.

Marcus, a ten-year-old, reportedly "forgets" to do his work or to study for a test or to turn in his homework. When asked why, he explains that he can't help it. Still, he does well in school. There are no complaints about his behavior in school. Teachers know he is a bright student, albeit an underachiever, who is able to pass his courses. At home, he is a different kid. He gets angry easily at the least thing that does not go his way or frustrates him. He then screams, yells, talks back, curses and insults parents, slams doors, and breaks things. Typically, if anything goes wrong, he blames his parents.

According to his parents, he was not always like this, but, he seems to have gotten worse as time went on. At the beginning, they took his "rebelliousness" as a sign of his being a strong and rather spunky child who needed love and understanding more than anything else. Over time, he became a handful, particularly when he "accidentally" hit or pushed his mom.

Generally speaking, much of a child's fearful, thoughtless, disruptive, and oppositional behavior can be best understood in terms of the unintended

> **Takeaway #8**
>
> **Overlooking repeated misbehavior functions as tacit approval and further encourages it.**

outcomes of parenting practices. In a word, their well-meaning efforts to deal with misbehavior tend to maintain inappropriate behavior.

Parents are talk-oriented . . .

First for the good news. Good parents want to help. They like to talk to and encourage a child to openly express feelings and concerns. They make every effort to console and soothe an imperious child by redoubling their loving efforts. Most parents give plenty of good speeches and heartfelt advice on responsibility and respect. They also discuss with a child how important it is that he should quit misbehaving so that everyone can feel less stressed. Certainly, it is important that parents explain to children that they have a responsibility to the family and to themselves. Admittedly, all these efforts are valuable and particularly useful with some children.

Words are very important particularly because there is evidence that a child's growth in verbal skills is highly dependent on the parent's own use of words at home. Verbal skills also correlate with academic success in school. Also, effective social interaction depends largely on verbal skills. That's why frequent talking to kids must be included in the daily parent-child interaction.

In general, encouraging frequent child-parent communication often garners the desired response. However, this approach is of limited value with a child who seems to be constantly testing parental resolve. Under these circumstances, parents find themselves repeating the same reminders and warnings ("I'll count to 10, and if you don't stop playing with the computer, I'm going to take it away for a week!") all of which are ignored by a difficult child.

Many of you already know that with a difficult child all the talking and discussing in the world seldom results in the desired change. The question is, "What can a loving parent do when reason and logic fail to persuade a stubborn and resistant child to change the way he acts?" Once again, the answer is, "plenty."

Here is some encouraging information: It is not that children are simply stubborn, difficult, and impervious to instructions. Rather, the instructional method chosen to teach a child has emphasized words to help a child change.

. . . but children are action-oriented.

Talking and reasoning are abstract and fleeting, and can go in one ear and out the other. Actions involve physical movement, and are dynamic and interactive. Actions are concrete and leave a "trace" in the environment when they have taken place. If a child says he put away his shoes in the closet, but they are still in the TV room, it is easier for Mom to know if the child followed her instructions.

Further, children learn largely through hands-on experiences, that is to say, by doing. Generally, what a child does has an effect on his immediate environment. Basically, a child discovers that his action often has a specific impact on his immediate physical environment in that it changes it in some recognizable way. An example would be playing with a toy where a child presses a button and finds out that doing so produces a movement or a sound. The kinetic response of the toy delights him and encourages him to keep playing.

However, when pressing a button no longer produces the movement or sound, he grows bored, stops playing with the toy, and moves on to another activity. In other words, when his action has no effect on his immediate physical environment he quits interacting with it and looks for alternative stimulation. Similarly, if what he does has little or no effect on how his parents interact with him, he gets bored, quits, and goes on to something else. On the other hand, he is more likely to repeat actions that parents cannot help paying attention to, or that reward or work for him.

Children play, do, act, and react, and thereby learn about their world and surroundings. This is how such experiences become knowledge. Similarly, children learn about the body and what it can do through movement, pushing, pulling, running, jumping, doing cartwheels, and so on. They find out that they are fast or slow as they play ball with their peers. These experiences give them a large fund of knowl-

---

 Tip #2 | **To develop self-esteem, encourage skill development in sports, dancing, playing musical instruments, and/or academic performance.**

---

edge of a non-verbal kind. It is through practice of these largely non-verbal activities including playing a musical instrument, dancing, and the arts in general that a child gradually develops his/her own sense of self-awareness and self-esteem.

Parents are lax on their follow-through.

Parents sabotage their own instructions to a child when they do not follow through on their own words. A mom might say, "You'd better quit watching TV and finish your home-work or you will not be allowed to go out and play," and later on allow the child to go out and play despite the fact that he has not finished his homework. Parents mean well, but the reality is that they are busy with their jobs, house-hold chores, and financial demands. Consequently, they do not have the time to physically take care of everything. In-stead, they try to stop some undesirable behavior by repeat-ing reminders, naggings, and threats to take things away.

A child has heard these words before, and his experience tells him that parental threats are often just a lot of words.

 Tip #3 | **Do what you said you were going to do. If you have threatened to take something away, limit the absence or suspension of privileges to one hour, or even half a day, then review the results of your actions**

Mom feels guilty about not being more available to her child and cannot bring herself to go through with her threats.

Parents are in the future . . . but children are in the here-and-now.

Parents are often frustrated by a child's seeming inability to think ahead, and to realize that some things you have to wait for. On a vacation trip, a parent may be asked incessantly, "Are we there yet?" A child appears not to un-derstand that it is going to take some time to get to a desti-nation. Sometimes, parents warn a child that he has to do better in school or he won't get a good job when he leaves school. Other times, after spanking their child, parents often add, "I know I'm doing this for your own good, and someday, you will understand and thank me for it." Similar comments are made by parents to explain why the child is not getting what he wants today but that someday he probably will understand.

For a child, all this is rather confusing. He's not thinking of the future. He lives in the present, and for him that's all he ever makes direct contact with. He wants what he wants when he wants it. Typically, he wants it, NOW! And typically he gets it too! His experience with his parents persuades him that that's how things work.

Today's child is oriented toward getting, not giving.

Problematic children are oriented toward immediate material gratification. They are consumers "par excellence." Their acquisition mania starts early and without anyone giving it a thought. For example, the fast food industry often promotes this by including plastic cards, little cars, and junk in general that kids get along with their order of burger and fries. Kids will demand to go eat at such places just to get these freebies and end up not eating because they are not hungry. They just want the stuff. Over time, as kids get jaded with the same freebies, the fast food industry introduces new junk which attracts kids once again to repeat the same cycle. And, so it goes.

A recent Gallup poll showed that when asked to rate what was most important to them, over half the number of children stated that it was money. And, indeed, they need it since they want to buy an endless number of computer games, DVDs, videos, and so on. Having the latest computer games, the right cell phone, iPod, and the right "stuff" (the right shoes, jeans, and so on) gets them immediate recognition from their peers. In their minds, they only have to acquire stuff to be cool, look good, and be deserving of respect.

While parents may not be sure what is going on with a child, they are painfully aware of the repetitive character of his demands, lack of cooperation, defiant attitude, and lack of consideration of others. In short, a difficult child often behaves in a socially insensitive and irresponsible manner.

We have invested much in our children's lives and worked very hard to give them everything we never had, or to make their childhood better than ours was. Naturally, we want them to grow emotionally, remain physically healthy, and be academically competent. Yet, as the educational and skill demands increase, what was good enough training yesterday is not acceptable today. The media paints a grim picture of our world and the future, and to top it all off, Mom and Dad have to work harder to provide food, home, and all the goodies that are portrayed every second on television for our children. Indeed, parenting in the time of emotional, cultural, and economic changes adds pressure on parents to shield a child from being negatively affected by these changes.

At this point it would be a luxury to trace when and how the parental practices that impact on children's minds and behavior started to change. Instead, try to put that aside for the moment and focus on what YOU can do today to help your child:

1. stop creating disruption, conflict, and stress in your family, and,

2. deal with his own feelings of frustration and low self-esteem.

Children need structure.

At the outset, children need a home-based structure to feel safe. Children are more likely to get lost, not know what to do, make mistakes, feel stupid, and feel bad, when they are in an unfamiliar setting or structure. A museum, a church, a classroom, a restaurant, a bank, a neighbor's home, a school bus, are all different structures within which children are expected to act in a certain way. A difficult child is likely to be puzzled at the different reaction he gets for behaving in school as he does at home. Until he learns that some behaviors that are accepted at home are not necessarily acceptable in school, or in someone else's home, he is likely to find it a challenge to go from one setting to another. For some children this requires more effort than they are willing to make.

Socially related skills have a specific content and structure.

Summer camps and other training programs involving sports as well as the arts such as music, dancing, et cetera, provide a structure as well as the specific content of skills to be taught. A major bonus is the incidental teaching of social skills as part and parcel of such extracurricular efforts.

Similarly, a home often provides a built-in structure and a set of expectations of conduct that parents have for a child. The structure and house rules are defined by each family and involve getting up in the morning, going to bed at night, doing schoolwork, eating meals together, helping with household chores, and so on.

THE INCIDENTAL TEACHING OF SOCIALLY RELATED SKILLS

Home-based situations and activities serve as the media through which incidental teaching of social skills is accomplished. The incidental teaching of social skills starts with very concrete actions taken by parents, such as asking a child to say, "Please," "Thank you," "I'm sorry," as the situation demands. This incidental learning of polite and respectful manners takes place over time as the parents consistently coach the child. Lack of such manners is exacerbated when parents have little or no structure at home. For example, many parents do not have a designated time or place when the family shares a meal together. Some children eat in bed or in the family room watching TV while the parents eat in the kitchen. Other children have a varying mealtime schedule and also varying bedtimes. In the absence of a regular time and place for specific activities, there is greater probability for arguments and "misplaced" behavior to occur. For example, a child who does homework in front of the TV is less likely to do efficient work because the activities compete for his focus and attention. The net result is that a child is likely to develop bad study habits when he is distracted, unfocused, and not well organized.

A child does better when his home environment is structured.

Many families rediscover the wheel on a daily basis. Efforts to correct a child's misconduct or to encourage discipline are not likely to succeed in the absence of some kind of organization in the child's home. Parents do well by establishing a time to get up and get ready for school, a time to come home, a time to play, a time to do homework, a time to pursue his interests, a time for the family to regroup in the evening before or after supper, and a time to go to bed. Indeed, as noted in Ecclesiastes, "There is a time for everything, and a season for every activity under heaven…There is a time to embrace and a time to refrain…There is a time to be silent and a time to speak." Knowing the beginning, middle, and end of a process makes it possible for a child to adapt his behavior and to sustain the appropriate level of motivation to start and complete a variety of tasks that are of low interest to him. This approach does not have to run like a military school, but allows for flexibility as needed.

Many arguments between parent and child involve misplaced school-related items. A chain of nagging reminders, accusations, and counterproductive child-parent interactions starts in the morning because a child cannot find his schoolbag, books, or school assignments. In the absence of a designated time and place for him to meet expectations, his behavior is likely to be at the mercy of any event or distraction that will compete for his attention. Under such conditions, a child is likely to act inconsistently: sometimes he may do his homework or help with household chores, and at other times he may not. On the other hand, an organized, structured, home environment "sends" signals or "reminders" to a child as to where he keeps his school-related items, and where he does his homework, or practices

---

 Tip #4 | **To encourage getting organized, it is useful to set a time and place for child-related activities.**

---

his music. These "signals" give him a sense of sameness and security that is comforting and helpful to encourage him to do what needs to be done in a time frame that fits his developmental age and skills.

Is a child merely a fragrant pile of blubber? Or an active member of society? Are children reluctant to be children? Sometimes yes. Sometimes no. A child wants freedom within the stone wall of guidance.

Pola, age 10

CHAPTER THREE

GOOD AND BAD HABITS ARE ACQUIRED

The bond of child with parent is a basic one. Parent-child relations are built on the child's need for safety and emotional reassurance. As a child bonds with a parent he feels secure and begins to explore his immediate environment largely through play and acting out. Through hands-on experiences a child learns about the world around him and, over time, about himself. A child enjoys physical contact and close relationship with parents. S/he's often recognized and acknowledged for cute or positive behavior, but sometimes parent's personal attention is also likely to follow a child's annoying or unwanted behavior. As a child begins to grow, s/he also discovers that good and bad behaviors share a common effect: they help establish a special physical contact and up-close-and-personal connection with parents. In many ways, the same process that accounts for the early development of skills, social and otherwise, also underlies the development of misbehavior. Gradually, over time, a child develops a style of interaction that parents often describe as selfish, manipulative, and sneaky. This style works well for the child in that he gets away with it but at the cost of goodwill and harmony in the household.

When a child has difficulties in school it is likely that he needs additional coaching to complement a teacher's efforts on his behalf. For most children, a home is the natural place where countless opportunities arise to learn to follow instructions and comply with real-world demands. Such is the case when Mom asks a child to put away his shoes in the closet, help fold the clean clothes coming out of the clothes dryer, and other age-appropriate household chores.

Good behavior has its benefits . . .

Behaving well serves a child to connect to his parents as they provide him with emotional rewards involving hugs, kisses, pats on the head, and other positive expressions of love and affection. These personal benefits often include greater parent involvement in a child's sports and academic activities as well as social development. As he grows, he is made to feel emotionally secure because his parents are proud of him and his accomplishments and pleased to do things with him. In short, he is the focus of their love and concern and enjoys a warm relationship with, and emotional closeness to, his parents.

Access to goodies and privileges, such as TV, computer games, and the like, are also likely to be included among the benefits. For example, to maximize schoolwork, it is helpful to link completion of homework to access to a child's preferred electronic entertainment. A child's preferred activities should be optional and accessible, under certain circumstances, such as timely completion of homework and/or household chores.

Still, it is the effective, emotional rewards inherent in being the center of attention and concern that have a special lasting influence on a child's behavior and relationship to his parents.

. . . but, good behavior that goes unattended will soon stop.

A child who frequently misbehaves and exhausts his parents with inappropriate behavior is likely to be overlooked when he is quiet and busy with his own projects. At such times, Mom may feel it best to leave a good thing alone. After all, that is when Mom believes she is finally able to take a break and enjoy some well-deserved peace and quiet. The trouble with this practice is that after a while, in the absence of attention, a child will grow uncomfortable, listless, and give up behaving well and explore other avenues for fun and stimulation. That is when he is most likely to do something to bring Mom's attention to him and reconnect with her. In general, when appropriate behavior goes unacknowledged for some time, a child is most likely to give it up and explore inappropriate ones instead.

> **Takeaway #9**
>
> **A child learns how to emotionally connect with parents through misbehavior.**

Chucky was a healthy baby who cried about five hours a day, day-in and day-out despite all efforts to soothe him. The pediatrician diagnosed him as suffering from infant colic. Typically this condition lasts about three to five months. There is no known medical basis or medical cure for it. Some parents find it reassuring that the condition will be over in a few months. The trouble with waiting is that it prevents or severely delays the attachment and bonding between mother and infant. Another important issue, of course, is that the parents begin to feel tense, irritated, and stressed by the baby's constant crying. Whenever there is a pause or quiet moment, a harassed mom cannot help but leave him be for fear that he might start crying all over again. Of course, as soon as the baby resumes crying, Mom may let him cry for a few minutes and then picks him up to soothe him. The baby thus begins to associate crying with Mom's attention and soothing, while quiet periods are associated with no attention and little or no stimulation. In a sense, this process unwittingly encourages a baby to cry to be close to Mommy.

That's why, with Chucky, it was important to consider an alternative approach to the problem. A good deal of research has been done regarding how infants learn. Babies less than two-weeks-old learn to connect and predict that one thing leads to another when two events occur very closely in time. Babies as young as one-week-old love musical sounds, as well as the experience of controlling events in their surroundings. This research led me to design a special routine, Comfort Training, to teach a colicky baby to self-sooth. First, Mom was advised to use a checklist throughout the day and take the appropriate steps if the baby was hungry, wet, had gas, or appeared physically ill. The goal was to have Mom teach the baby self-quieting skills. Basically, the idea was to reverse the colicky baby's experience that associated Mom's presence and cuddling with crying, and associated calm and quiet with boredom and no stimulation. Now, the baby got the music and Mom's stimulation (lots of touching, lots of happy talk) when he was calm and alert, but no music or stimulation for about 2-3 minutes when he cried. We found that when music was linked to calm behavior, the crying stopped. Chucky learned he could listen to music and have Mom come to him when he was calm. Simply having the same music available without linking it to the baby's behavior did not reduce the baby's crying: the baby continued crying. It was only when music and Mom's stimulation were associated with calm behavior that the baby stayed calm for long periods of time.

> **Takeaway #10**
>
> **Focus on appropriate behavior or you'll be focusing on inappropriate behavior.**

No untoward symptoms were observed even six months after this intervention. Mom and Dad were delighted with their baby.

Where have all the good manners gone?

Currently there appears to be a heightened awareness of the lack of children's good manners. At one time, parents and teachers were relied upon to teach social amenities and respect for others. Today, social practices have changed dramatically on a variety of fronts including the way kids dress and the way they talk to parents, teachers, and older people. In the absence of social training at home, few avenues remain to show kids how to behave in a civil manner.

We have all witnessed children whose behavior in public shows social insensitivity and blatant disrespect for the rights of others. To get a child's attention and to stop, or at least decrease, problematic behaviors, parents are often reduced to frequent scolding, yelling, and threats. Typically, these threats remain just words as they seldom are followed by parental action. Soon, a child will defy and challenge parents to the point of the parents' exhaustion. Parents will then resort to placating a child with bribes ("OK, I'll buy you an ice-cream cone if you stop teasing your brother). Sometimes, they may actually do the task the child was asked to do in the first place, just to keep a semblance of peace at home. At other times, parents are apt to overlook offensive behavior, and dismiss bullying behavior to achieve a short-term goal: peace in the family. Simply ignoring unwanted behavior, however, has its downside.

Naughty Nina, an eleven-year-old

Dad is reading the newspaper sitting in his favorite chair while Nina is slouched over the couch doing nothing in particular. When Mom came into the room to ask if someone could give her a hand, Dad told Nina to help her mom, but Nina answered, "Why should I do it? Why don't YOU do it?"

Parents often assume that children from the age of four already understand the language and should be able to follow instructions. Yet, there is a good deal of instructions and parental commands that children do not seem to be able to process or, at least, are not motivated to act upon. In the meantime, a lot of yelling and nagging takes place to assure a kid's compliance with parental instructions to no avail.

Behaving poorly has its benefits too!

When a child experiences his parents as too busy to notice him, or too indifferent to his needs, concerns, or accomplishments, he is likely to gradually lose motivation to behave appropriately. A child who feels unappreciated, unfairly treated, or stressed-out may become uncooperative, and exhibit some dramatic behavior that stops his parents in their tracks, compelling them to finally focus their attention on him. As a child is "asking for it" his parents will redouble their efforts to "straighten him out," and to remind and nag him to assume responsibility for his actions.

Parents will do so either by scolding, disciplining, or just plain shouting and threatening with punishment. To a child who feels misunderstood, overlooked, or neglected, any attention—even if it is negative—is better than none. The net result, then, is that a "needy" child may get exaggerated parental attention whether he misbehaves or behaves appropriately. Not surprisingly, this often results in his having good days and terrible days. Parents often describe such patterns of behavior as having a Doctor Jekyll and Mr. Hyde quality!

The parents of Arnie, a five-year-old boy, shared the general belief that children are like flowers that flourish naturally if you don't tamper with them. Arnie was an expressive, sharp little boy who was liked in school. He made friends, had fun in school, and his teachers were pleased with his conduct. However, Arnie's parents had a special problem. They were prisoners in their own home. They could not leave home on weekends, nor could they leave Arnie with a babysitter. The last time they engaged a babysitter so that they could attend a party, Arnie ran out of the house and parked himself in front of the family's car so that Dad could not leave the garage without first running over his own child! No amount of reasoning, reassurance, or rewards could lift the anxiety and fear that Arnie seemed to develop when his parents told him that they would only be away for a little while. An emotional drama was provoked when his parents indicated they wanted to go out. For the last six months his parents had rarely been out as a couple alone or to visit with friends. Matters came to a head when Arnie did not want to allow Dad to attend the Braves baseball game in town although, as Dad pointed out, he had paid dearly for advance tickets to the ballgame. That did it! Dad decided right there and then to consult a psychologist.

Review the way you deal with your child's challenges.

Parents need to review the way they deal with a child's daily challenges. Sometimes, parents unwittingly send mixed messages to a child regarding discipline and adherence to the family's values. Indeed, while parents' resolve may be firm and decisive, their follow-through may be inconsistent, and at worst, non-existent.

As a result, some children seem to revert to earlier stages of development in that they act like younger versions of themselves in need of more cuddling, emotional, and even physical support. Parents find themselves dressing the child, allowing bedtimes to not be enforced, becoming a child's assistants to find schoolbooks, staying next to the child while he dawdles over his homework, and so on. Parents try to spare a child any bad times and offer to help whenever possible. In spite of the parents' efforts to create and maintain a peaceful, calm household, the child often remains surly, resistant, and unwilling to accept the help as intended. As a consequence, parents often redouble their efforts to be helpful and, at some point, find themselves in conflict: they cannot win for losing. Often, parents are caught in a routine of dealing with scenes and displays of temper and entitlement and merely give in to save their child and themselves from a frustrating and highly emotional situation. Parents do everything they can to avoid upsetting their child for fear that doing so might have a negative effect on the child's personality.

Takeaway #11

Placating a demanding child encourages more demanding behavior.

What seemed to have happened to Arnie, who did not allow his parents to leave the house, is that he gradually, almost imperceptibly, came to control his parents' movements. For example, at one time when Mom went to the mailbox to pick up the mail, Arnie fussed, screamed, and cried so much that Mom avoided this emotional scene by either taking Arnie with her or checking the mailbox after Arnie had gone to bed.

Parents worry that they will somehow hurt their children emotionally if they allow a child to have direct contact with the consequences of his actions. Over time, the parents' pervasive guilt develops the child's "can do no wrong" style of behavior. As such, a child feels that Mom or Dad will take care of him, no matter how badly he behaves. These children develop a sense of not having to be responsible for themselves. They may participate in a variety of projects, for example, but after attending once or twice, decide to quit because the activity is boring and they want to do something else. By that time, the parent may have paid a registration fee for a special ballet class or baseball camp that cannot be refunded. As the children in these situations have nothing to lose nor are they inconvenienced by dropping out of a given activity, they may even be puzzled when asked why they want to quit the program they had previously insisted they wanted to join. For them, "it's no big deal." All the speeches they may hear from their parents about the need to be responsible are really like background noise.

The "material child" wants things that he quickly devalues only to go back to the mall to get more stuff. He behaves as if he were sampling the goods and once he does, he is no longer interested in them. Considerations involving money or inconvenience to his parents do not enter his mind. He may change his mind about a special item or program his parents paid hard-earned money for on some trivial basis, such as, "I did not know it was going to be like this." If the child has no stake on whether he chooses one course of action versus another, he never learns to weigh his options or to develop a sense of personal responsibility.

As a child grows disruptive, uncaring, irresponsible, and argumentative despite all corrective efforts, parents often choose to blame the powerful influences of school, peers, music, and the media. By so doing, however, they are essentially giving up their responsibility as parents and the only opportunity to act as agents of change in their children's lives. During a child's formative years, home is still the place where social and work-related behaviors are learned, practiced, and developed in a climate of love and understanding. When parents look for reasons outside of the home environment, they surrender to the inevitable loss of control and influence over their child's behavior.

The past is gone but actions in the present will affect the future.

From time to time, parents express their sense of helplessness about what to do. As one mother put it, "We have made mistakes with Susan but we can't change the past. We tried everything and nothing seems to work. We just have to live with it." Actually, there is no reason for parents to simply tolerate and live with difficult-to-change behaviors. It's true that parents cannot change the past, but they can work in the present to affect the child's future behavior. After all, the present is the only stage in which family interactions can be examined and modified. Understanding the current circumstances surrounding problematic behavior empowers parents to marshal their own resources for change by managing the daily, meaningful consequences of a child's behavior.

Parent and child have a reciprocal influence.

A family is a dynamic social system wherein each member affects one another through consequences they provide to each other in their familial interactions. This is the process through which parents influence their children. It is also the same process through which children influence their parents' behavior. For example, through his own experience with his parents, a child may learn that Mom is the disciplinarian.

On the other hand, through their own experience with their son, Dad may think that his son needs a lot of reassurance while Mom may regard her son as needing a firm hand. The point is that sometimes each parent may "read" a child's behavior differently and therefore react and provide different consequences for the same behavior. This often results in a child favoring the least demanding rather than the more demanding parent, and generally neutralizing or defeating efforts at parental control.

Again, it must be noted that neither a child nor his parents act according to some pre-arranged plan that systematically attempts to change one another's behavior. Their actions take place outside of their awareness, at the doing, behavioral level rather than at the thinking, cognitive level. This means that child and parent learn to behave toward one another in a spontaneous manner with little thought given to the actual effect of their interaction on one another's behavior. In this way, the child and parent mutually influence one another's behavior and well being through their daily interactions.

***

Debbie, a four-year-old, needed much reassurance and nurturance from her parents. Each morning when Mom went to work, Debbie ran up to her at the door and cried, moaned, and pleaded with her mother to please not leave her. Mom spent some time consoling her and explaining that she loved her dearly, but that she needed to go to work and that Grandma would stay with her. Debbie insisted that Mom stay with her and the more Mom tried to reassure her and soothe her, the more intense was Debbie's emotional upheaval.

This daily routine took a lot out of the mother because by the time she finally left for work, she felt emotionally drained. What made things more difficult to understand was that as soon as Mom was out of sight, Debbie quit moaning and crying and busied herself with her toys.

Because she worked outside of the home, Mom worried, felt guilty, and felt responsible for Debbie's "fears of abandonment." Mom was coached to remain loving and sensitive to her child's feelings and to leave for work with a short explanation, a kiss, and a hug. To avoid additional distress, she was to leave the house without looking back. Withholding the explanations and soothing when Debbie cried, resulted in a drastic reduction in the seemingly uncontrollable emotional reaction to her mom's going to work. Within a short time Debbie was playing with her toys and interrupted her fun just long enough to give a hug and a kiss to Mommy as she left for work.

***

Jimmy, a four-year-old boy, delights in teasing his mom by pulling her purse while they are shopping. Typically, he ignores his mom's repeated requests to stop pulling her purse. Finally, Mom's reaction becomes firm, loud, and intense. Jimmy stops pulling the purse, but within a few minutes he is at it again. Mom again asks him to stop pulling her purse or else he is asking for trouble. By pulling her purse, Jimmy keeps Mom's attention focused on him, and, by so doing, Mom feeds this type of interaction. Still, Mom's purse is not the issue. The purse is only the means to connect with Mom. Jimmy connects with Mom through misbehaving. Should he stop pulling Mom's purse, the game would end there and so would the connection with Mom. It is to his benefit to continue to misbehave to maintain that connection.

Mom's reaction to Jimmy's annoying pattern of behavior influences whether he repeats or does not repeat the same behavior. As Mom is fully engaged and feeding energy back to Jimmy, he has a bright smile on his face. While all this is going on, child and mother have spent more time interacting with each other than might be the case otherwise.

A child's actions influence parental behavior.

Fundamentally, a child influences parental behavior by the way he acts toward them. Often, he has learned a variety of behavioral and emotional ways of expressing himself from interaction with his parents, peers, and teachers. What he learns from his social environment is, again, largely influenced by the personal cost/benefit consequences linked to his behavior. For example, a child will favor his parents with attention, approval, affection, or acknowledgement, when they comply with his requests. However, a child will become silent, sad, or angry when parents do not do his bidding. Typically, a child will attempt to neutralize and override parental resolve by adopting an aggressive posture or resentful attitude that controls and dominates what the family does at a particular time and place. Often, parents use the words manipulation and emotional blackmail to describe what they feel a child is doing to them, as exemplified by the following actions:

GROWING DEAF

Children ignore parental requests to start some action such as pick up their toys, books, and so on. They act as if they never heard Mom's reminders. Ignoring parental requests or instructions often works for a child. Parents are likely to get annoyed and tired of issuing reminders and decide to do the child's task themselves.

GROWING COLD

A child's relationship with a parent, be it positive or negative, influences a parent's behavior. Sometimes, children withhold their affection, act "cold," indifferent, or show disapproval of their parents. When they so behave, parents feel so uncomfortable that they are likely to indulge their children in an effort to find relief. At other times, parents placate their children by reducing their expectations of the child.

GROWING DISTANT

Sometimes, children do not acknowledge parental responsibility and authority over them. At such times, children may actively avoid interacting with their parents or actively disengage from any ongoing interaction with them. For example, Kerry, came home from school, hardly said hello to Mom, went to his room, and announced he wanted to be left alone. Most parents are emotionally affected by such actions because they produce feelings of discomfort, anger, conflict, or guilt.

A child trains parents to accept problematic behavior.

The repetitive problematic behavior of a child can lead his parents to accept a gradual increase in disobedience and emotional acting-out. Often, adults will come to regard such a child as someone to simply accept or ignore. This means that disobedience, boorish, and generally uncivil behavior are overlooked, tolerated, finally excused, and, in effect, accepted. Generally speaking, the style of behavior of a difficult child tends to create excessive stress on the fabric of family life.

A divorced mother reports that her eleven-year-old daughter Ronnie acts like she does not care about her. Whenever she tries to interest her daughter in going to a concert or a special event, Ronnie asks, with a suffering look, "Do I have to go, Mom?" A couple of times, when she took her to watch a ballet performance, it did not take long before Ronnie demanded to go home. According to her mother, things have gotten to the point where Ronnie seems to have veto power on any activities selected by her mother.

Ronnie's behavior illustrates the process that leads parents to adjust to a child's problematic behavior by lowering their expectations and standards of conduct to avoid endless arguments and emotional confrontations.

Child-parent relations are regulated by an interactive feedback loop.

The reciprocal character of child-parent interaction throws light on what "causes" a child to behave in certain ways. This reciprocal social influence is illustrated when a child's behavior is so disruptive that his parents will get into an emotional confrontation or give in to his demands. In a short time, this negative pattern of child-parent interaction is repeated: both child and parent are stuck in their emotional interactions with one another.

Dreamy Doreen's situation, discussed previously, illustrates how a child and mother influence each other's behavior. Every school day she missed the school bus and Mom had to drive her to school. Here, the daily problem may no longer be possible to trace to Doreen without including Mom in the mix. Again, because their influence is reciprocal, a solution was found by altering the way they interacted with one another over the school bus issue. Therefore, blaming a parent or a child is neither fair nor helpful.

Rather, the focus here is on promoting a loving, cooperative, and respectful "culture" at home through child-parent interactions involving the unlearning of problematic emotional behaviors and the learning of more positive ones.

CHAPTER FOUR

THE STRATEGIC APPROACH
TO PROBLEMATIC BEHAVIOR

Children are social beings acting on a social stage. Generally, as they enjoy being the center of attention, they seek parental approval. However, at other times, when feeling conflicted and fearful, they act to escape or avoid emotionally difficult situations at home or in other social settings.

A child's behavior does not take place in a vacuum. Remember, a child's behavior is intimately connected to his or her social context. Places or settings such as home, school, and/or public areas represent the social context within which a child's behavior is most susceptible to social influence. From this perspective a child's problematic behavior influences and is influenced by his social environment, primarily, his parents.

A strategic approach goes beyond the description of problematic behavior alone to a description of its effects on the behavior of those around the child, particularly Mom and Dad. Fundamentally, an analysis of problematic behavior is concerned with interactional episodes involving child and parent. Although problematic behavior may have developed early on in interaction with the family, it is the prevailing pattern of parent-child interaction that often continues to influence a child. As these two-way interactions occur with relatively predictable regularity, both child and parent come to know and anticipate what the other will say and do. In other words, parent and child read one another like a book. Their moves toward one another are practically choreographed. Each affects the other by repeating the same negative behavior, emotional tone, and intensity toward one another. They are stuck in a negative feedback cycle.

Mom may be heard complaining to her son, "What's the matter with you? How many times do I have to remind you to start your homework when you come home, and not wait until I come home from work to do it?" Given that Mom can almost predict what her child is going to do, What's the use of reminding him? Why does she bother? What is the point? Mom's answer is, "What else can I do? I've got to do something!" Indeed, in the absence of a known solution, Mom cannot help but repeat what she knows in hopes that someday her son may change. Here, hope springs eternal.

The emerging negative feelings from these repeated encounters may be viewed as collateral emotional responses also susceptible to social influence.

Paradoxically, even well-meaning efforts to resolve negative interactions tend to maintain them. Such was the case with five-year-old Heidi whose loving parents "tuned in"' most actively and emotionally to soothe and nurture her when she "pitched a fit." When things did not go exactly the way she wanted, Heidi went into an awful emotional meltdown. Her parents recognized the effect she had on them and lovingly dubbed her the "Drama Queen."

What would it take to end this steady, and repetitive, negative cycle? What it would take is for either parent or child to simply behave differently so as not to feed into one another's expectations. That, of course, is easier said than done. Still, experience suggests that it may be easier for parents, as the adults, to take the first step in that direction.

The approach taken here focuses on altering the natural consequences that typically follow unwanted behavior. These consequences are provided by parents in response to a child's misbehavior. These consequences are an integral part of the specific parenting practices aimed at correcting a child's "problem." Paradoxically, it is these natural parenting practices that unwittingly invite and encourage a child's "problem." Therefore, the goal here is to transform these parenting practices into a motivational engine that turns a child's problem into its own solution.

ANATOMY OF MISBEHAVIOR

The emphasis of the strategic approach is on the characteristics of problematic behavior and of the social context within which it emerges. Accordingly, this approach looks into three major areas that often influence the occurrence and maintenance of problematic behavior: 1) context of misbehavior; 2) parental reaction to misbehavior; and, 3) the personal cost/benefit linked to misbehavior.

1. Context that cues and triggers misbehavior

   a. Place: Where is the problematic behavior most likely to occur? (for example, while riding in the family's car, etc.)

   b. Time: When is it most likely to occur? (in the morning, at meal time, etc.)

   c. Social triggers. What seems to trigger it? (Being asked to help with chores, waiting, not getting what s/he wants

This analysis often includes finding out the social circumstances, such as who is around at the time (peers, parents, teachers, strangers) when the problematic behavior occurs. Also, it is just as important to find out where and when problematic behavior does NOT occur, or is least likely to occur.

2. Parental reaction to misbehavior

   a. Do parents often react to correct and teach a child socially appropriate behavior? Yes or No

   b. Do parents often react emotionally, laugh, argue, or remind a child of his responsibilities? Yes or No

   c. Do parents restrict, or penalize a child for his misbehavior? Yes or No

Certain consequences involving cost/benefit flow naturally from misbehaving. In addition to the social attention that misbehavior commands, parents may enable a child to avoid doing unpleasant or effortful tasks by making excuses for his failure to follow instructions or by reducing, and sometimes eliminating, their level of expectations.

3. The personal cost/benefit link to misbehavior

a. Is there personal cost for inappropriate behavior? Yes or No

b. Is there personal benefit for appropriate behavior? Yes or No

Generally speaking, the most effective way to discourage inappropriate behavior is through exacting a personal cost while at the same time encouraging and nurturing appropriate behavior by linking it to personal benefits.

A STEP-BY-STEP CHECKLIST TO HELP YOU EXAMINE WHAT IS GOING ON WITH A CHILD

Use the following checklist to help you find out what may be going on with a child. Look for answers to the following questions: What does he do? Where? When? What happened as a result of his misbehavior?

1. **What does he do?**

He procrastinates in his schoolwork and drags it on every night. He must have his mom next to him to do the work.

2. **Where?**

In his room (at the kitchen table, in front of the

TV, computer, and so on)

3. When?

Every day during school days

4. What happens when he acts that way?

Mom takes a good deal of time to explain to him the importance of doing well in school. She also sits next to him to encourage him to do his work.

He persists in procrastinating, so that he is still working on his homework at bedtime. Mom has to coax him to go to bed so that he can get enough sleep.

5. Is there a time and place when he does NOT procrastinate? Are certain people present during those times?

He doesn't procrastinate when he is practicing the trumpet for school band.

What happens then?

Mom leaves him alone, and busies herself with her own tasks.

6. What does the child gain or lose by procrastinating?

It would seem that Mother's attention and physical closeness is the major benefit for him. On the other hand, the possibility is that if he quit his procrastination Mom might no longer be focused on his activities. Soon, that would likely result in his going back to his old procrastinating ways which once again would "call" for Mom's attention and closeness.

ANATOMY OF CHILD MANAGEMENT

To increase interest and cooperation from a problematic child it is useful to employ a motivational system. The motivational point system consists of three steps all of which can be described in performance terms as follows:

1. Select a task and give clear instructions as to how it is to be completed.

"Ned will vacuum and clean the common areas when he returns from school, and, before Mom arrives home at 4:30 p.m."

"Shauna will complete daily school work after supper and before the eight o'clock TV show that she wants to watch."

2. Establish consequences based on a child's preferences, likes, and dislikes.

Ned and Shauna may choose from a menu of privileges and rewards agreed upon by child and parent. For example, a child may select to watch TV, play with the computer, talk on the phone, go to the mall with friends, stay up late, invite a friend over, and so on.

3. Establish a linkage between a child's completion of an assigned task (in socially appropriate ways) and its consequences (personal cost and personal benefit).

A motivational system involves consequences that represent a benefit to a child for behaving appropriately, and a cost for behaving inappropriately. For example, a child earns 30 minutes of TV when he assists doing the dishes, but does not earn it when he fails to finish his chore. If he finishes his chore without arguing and complaining, he earns an additional 30 minutes for a total of one hour of TV viewing. If he finishes his chore but complains the whole time he is doing the chore, he earns 80 percent of the privilege. For example, he would earn about 24 minutes instead of 30 minutes of TV. In short, there is an incentive for doing his chore and for behaving in socially appropriate ways, and a disincentive for failing to do his chore or doing it while behaving badly toward others.

AN ADDITIONAL SOURCE OF POSITIVE BEHAVIOR

A relatively easy opportunity to develop positive behavior patterns is found in the instances when a child does NOT misbehave. At such times, you can encourage and nurture those "hidden" behaviors through spontaneously selected natural consequences. For example, when the child is reading quietly or playing with his toys, go over and give him a hug.

THE MOTIVATIONAL SYSTEM

The expression "Different strokes for different folks!" suggests that people are motivated by different things. Indeed, for a motivational system to be effective, it must include a wide range of events and activities any or all of which are child-oriented and may serve as incentives or reinforcers. Failure to do so will result in a low level of motivation or interest which would make it more difficult to prompt a child to engage in appropriate behavior.

Most reinforcers may be subsumed under four somewhat overlapping types :

Social reinforcers include praise and, in general, social attention and concern. For example, social reinforcement may be experienced from peers' positive comments about one's skills or a teacher's comments regarding one's academic skills or about one's deportment. There are also physical reinforcers such as hugs, kisses, eye contact, a pat on the back, and the like.

As it happens, however, many socially reinforcing events or activities found in everyday situations involving the family grow into problematic behaviors; for example, a pre-adolescent boy who will not play ball unless his Dad practices with him, or a child who will not start her homework unless Mom sits by her side, or a young child who insists on having his mom read an ever-growing number of bedtime stories before he goes to sleep.

Social reinforcement has a powerful influence over the behavior of children, but used correctly and at the right time, social reinforcers nurture and strengthen good behavior rather than difficult behavior.

Material reinforcers include such items as toys, CDs, a new bike, a video, a special brand of jeans, a particular computer game, and so on. Material reinforcers can also be consumable items such as juice, chips, soft drinks, candy, and so on.

Activity reinforcers are more complex in that they involve opportunities to play outside, ride a bike, play the drums, rehearse baton twirling with friends, go on a hike to the mountains, and so on. Some teenagers stay up late at night to surf the net or watch TV, while others want to shop at the mall with friends or go to a movie. Special privileges can also be included here, such as the opportunity to have a friend overnight, the choice of certain clothes to wear, going to a rock concert with friends, and so on.

Symbolic reinforcers. Tokens (stars, points, credits) are items that bridge the gap between the time when a child engages in appropriate behavior and the opportunity to exchange the tokens for the back-up reinforcer. A child will be motivated to do well in school despite the fact that his favorite reinforcer, playing games on the computer, is not available until six hours later. A child's motivation develops naturally when she gains experience earning points (tokens, stars, etc.), through her own efforts and can exchange them for a wide range of back-up reinforcers made available by her parents at home. Under these conditions, a child is motivated to listen to her parents' requests. Further, she wants to meet parental expectations since failure to do so will result in earning no points, and therefore no back-up reinforcers.

Parents do not need money to motivate their children to behave appropriately in school, do their homework, help in the logistics of keeping the house clean, follow parental requests, and so on. They simply need to expose their children to symbolic consequences in the form of points that follow their cooperative versus uncooperative conduct. The point system allows a child to redeem these earned points for events, activities, and privileges of their choice. Soon, the point system becomes a powerful source of motivation that parents can employ to develop, regain, or enhance a child's cooperative and responsible behavior. Therefore, it is critical that parents be mindful of the potential for behavioral change that flows from their decision to grant, delay, or deny these reinforcers to a child.

Adjusting parental expectations, a child's behavior, and behavioral consequences is a dynamic process. At the outset, it is necessary that the expectations that a child and parent have of one another be described. This tactic consists of specifying the conditions under which a child's cooperative behavior will earn him access to agreed-upon incentives and privileges. A complementary tactic to reduce distrust and maximize mutual understanding is to have both parents and child specify in writing what a child's daily responsibilities are as well as the privileges that parents will grant for meeting these responsibilities. A written agreement protects a child from perceived ambiguous, capricious, or inconsistent house rules. It is also possible for the family to review their written agreement and clarify it in a timely manner when there is any doubt about these expectations.

Parents do well when they adjust their expectations as well as the incentives to a child's age, repertoire of skills, and social behavior. Just as important is to clarify that the self-selected privileges and incentives are dependent on a child completing the specified chore or task(s). For example, Ned's mother gave him permission to stay up after bedtime when he assisted with doing the dishes. Shauna's father allowed her to phone her friend when she finished her homework before 8:00 p.m.

Following are a few words of caution regarding child-parent agreements in the form of home contracts.

Home contracts help to articulate child-parent expectations and thereby avoid unnecessary misunderstandings. Also, they allow child and parent to fine-tune their interpretation of the meaning of chores or the worth of privileges.

Often, a child will sign any contract, despite all evidence that he has no intention to live up to the written agreement. This type of agreement or "contract" between parent and child has little intrinsic value by itself. One should not expect a child to change just because he has agreed to meet a particular set of expectations.

The effectiveness of any agreement derives from the consequences provided by parents for adhering to the agreed-upon rules. It is this behavior-consequence linkage that "powers" adaptive interactional patterns in the family. Therefore, this linkage requires close monitoring by parents to assure that the agreement is working as intended. Problems are most likely to develop when parents neglect to verify the occurrence of the appropriate behavior or to provide consequences for adhering to or breaking the agreement.

Parental expectations of a child regarding chores should be age appropriate. A child should not be expected to slave away doing household chores or to assist in the completion of household chores in preference to doing homework. Further, the natural needs of a child to enjoy himself must be respected. A child's childhood should not be sacrificed so that he becomes the "virtual" parent or the "parentified" child responsible for household chores.

Sometimes, a child's inappropriate behavior is such that it requires more than reliance on positive reinforcement. The goal is to reduce inappropriate behavior but just as important is not to produce severe emotional reaction.

For example, Jesse, a teenager, earned extra points for catching the school bus on time. Typically, Jesse exchanged points to call her friends in the evening. However, when she missed her school bus she did not have enough points to exchange for the phone privilege. Two distinct advantages derived from this strategy. The first one is that Jesse became more actively involved in catching the bus on a regular basis to avoid losing her phone privileges. The second one is that Jesse's mother also benefited from Jesse's behavior change since she was spared all the shouting, screaming, and emotional stress that went with reminding her daughter to be on time for the school bus.

THE FORM AND FUNCTION OF PROBLEMATIC BEHAVIOR

A myriad of behavior patterns may be annoying to parents, such as a child whining, screaming, arguing, sulking, and so on. Other behaviors include slamming of doors, pounding the wall, door, throwing things. Clearly, each of these behaviors is different from one another. Yet, although the form of these behaviors is varied, they all share the same function: they annoy and disturb parents (teachers and others). For example, David teases his younger sister Mary every chance he gets. Sometimes he physically pushes her around or pulls her hair. These forms of behavior are only variations on the same theme, but the behaviors share the same function: they call for the parents to intercede on Mary's behalf.

THE PURPOSE OF PROBLEMATIC BEHAVIOR IS FOUND IN ITS SOCIAL CONTEXT

To paraphrase the bard: There's more to misbehavior than parents have ever dreamed of. In general, a child's problematic behavior serves two major purposes:

1. **One purpose of problematic behavior is to reduce or avoid discomfort and frustration.** For example, Andy constantly delayed and postponed doing his chores until finally Dad got tired of waiting, assumed that Andy had forgotten altogether, and proceeded to do the chores himself. In effect, "forgetting" or postponing doing what he was asked to do paid off in that Andy avoided work and inconvenience.

2. **The other purpose of problematic behavior is to gain and control parental attention and related benefits.** For example, whenever thirteen-year-old Linda did not get her way, she became defiant and "ugly" toward her parents. Often, she mocked them mercilessly and continued her disrespectful behavior until she succeeded in having one of her parents side with her.

Tantrums illustrate these two major "purposes." One purpose is to gain parental attention and related benefits. This is likely to happen when a child is bored, or experiencing insufficient social stimulation. Another purpose of a tantrum is to escape or reduce parental demands. This is likely to happen when parents ask a child to help with chores or to follow instructions.

The meaning of problematic behavior, then, can be found in the related cost/benefit to a child. When David teased Mary, his actions commanded parental attention that unwittingly further encouraged his problematic behavior. So, what is the meaning behind David's persistent annoying? While it could be said that the meaning is to be found in the social reaction provoked by David's annoying behavior, even David would find it difficult to be consciously aware of it.

Finally, it should be noted that in replacing misbehavior with appropriate behavior we are actually changing the meaning of a child-parent interaction from a conflicting to a more benign one for both the child and the parent.

Exaggerated helplessness connects a child to his family.

When he experiences a social and emotional disconnect at home, a child is more likely to engage in dramatic behaviors that cause parents to stop whatever they are doing and run to help the child. By becoming the focus of his parents' love and concern, a child may experience a kind of an emotional reconnection to his family. In the future, under similar circumstances, he is likely to behave in dramatic ways because, in the past, he has found relief and felt reconnected to his parents by so behaving. This does not mean that a child has reasoned this out. Rather, it is the personal cost-benefit process associated with problematic behavior that may favor its reoccurrence. Often, the effect of this process alone is sufficiently robust to account for the development and maintenance of problematic behavior and associated thoughts and feelings.

Johnny one-note: "Mom, I forgot my trombone at home (again)."

Elaine is a lawyer, and the single parent of thirteen-year-old Johnny. She reports she can no longer deal with her son's irresponsibility.

"He drives me nuts with the irresponsible things he does and it's like all the time. To give you an idea, yesterday he called me at work saying he had forgotten his trombone and band was his very next class. When I told him I had an important brief I was working on, he stopped me by saying he'd be dropped from the band if he didn't have his instrument! So, of course, I had to leave my office, drive all the way home, pick up that blasted trombone, and take it all the way across town to his high school. He's just irresponsible!

"But, that's not all. He says he's going to clean his room and he doesn't. He says he's going to mow the lawn, but he runs out of time and just does not get it done. Things like that. But, really I can live with that sort of thing. What I cannot keep doing is leaving work to get his trombone for him! Now, mind you, he's a good boy, but I can't help getting mad at him because this is not the first time he's forgotten his trombone. Oh no! But if I told him once, I told him a thousand times. But he just can't seem to remember. I don't know what it is. My Granny, who's from the Georgia mountains, would have described Johnny as a "sorry mess." What on Earth can I do with him to make him understand? I mean, how is he going to handle college when the time comes? You know what I'm saying?"

A FUNCTIONAL (PURPOSE-DRIVEN) STRATEGY FOR BEHAVIOR CHANGE: IDENTIFYING TYPICAL CIRCUMSTANCES RELATED TO PROBLEMATIC BEHAVIORS

A child's problematic behavior cannot be understood independent of the cost-benefit unique to the family (social) context within which it occurs. Therefore, it is useful for parents to learn to identify the typical circumstances associated with a child's problematic behavior. What follows are the specific steps that parents can take in that regard.

1. Check when, and, where the problematic behavior typically occurs. Is it more likely at home, at school, in public places?

2. Check what he gets out of misbehaving to uncover his "purpose" in so behaving. What does he gain? What does he avoid?

3. Check for early patterns of repetitive misbehavior and their consequences. Have there been some special emotional events for this behavior early in the development of a child?

4. Check the types of typical consequences being used to influence his behavior. For example, parents often take things away from a child and/or "ground" him for a few days. At other times they placate him by giving in to his demands.

An Analysis of the Irresponsible Behavior of Johnny One-Note, a Thirteen-Year Old

Rather than thinking that Johnny is irresponsible because of his personality, or because he is angry at his mother, we are going to look at the circumstances that prevail in school and at home when he forgets his trombone.

In school, what does the music teacher do about it?

As it happened, Johnny's teacher had reminded him twice that he would be dropped from the band next time he failed to bring his instrument to class.

At home, does he discuss the problem with his mom and what does Mom actually do when he leaves his trombone at home?

Mom reported that she and Johnny had many discussions about the importance of assuming responsibility for one's actions. Generally, Johnny argued and defended himself by saying that he had a lot on his mind and could not remember everything. He wondered why everyone made such a big deal of this.

How did Johnny solve the problem?

He solved his forgetfulness problem in school by promising the music teacher he would take care of the matter. At home, he took care of the problem by handing the problem over to his mother's care.

What is the cost/benefit to Johnny of forgetting his trombone at home?

The personal cost (in effort and organized behavior on his part) is minimal: he only has to make a phone call to his mom and ask for help. On the other hand, Johnny's personal benefit is that he gets his trombone without additional work or worry on his part. It could be said that Johnny's irresponsible behavior has been unwittingly developed and maintained through Mom's enabling efforts.

Analysis Of Reciprocal Influence: Johnny and his Mother

Why does Johnny's mother persist in going out of her way to help him when it is so inconvenient for her to do so?

The answer lies in their reciprocal influence. Therefore, the same analysis we used to understand why Johnny is so forgetful is useful to understand Mother's rescue efforts. Specifically, what does Mother gain or avoid by rescuing Johnny each time he forgets his trombone? Admittedly, she helps him because Johnny is her son, she loves him, and so she's only doing what a loving mother would do. Also, Mother does not want Johnny to be upset with her, so she helps him. On the other hand, what would happen if she ignored his plea for help? For one thing, she would feel awful and guilty if she did not help her child when he most needed her. In addition, she could not stand having Johnny be angry with her for not helping. Therefore, when he calls her at work to get his trombone, she leaves work, goes home, finds the trombone, takes it to school, and then drives back to work. The reciprocal feature of such interactions assures that a child and his parents will behave toward one another so as to reduce or eliminate annoying and emotionally difficult interactions.

In practical terms it means that close observation of these interactions over time allows parents to gauge the reciprocal influence they and the child have on one another's behavior. Johnny's forgetfulness and irresponsibility are not the result of problems at the cognitive level. There is no brain problem here. Rather, Johnny behaves in this manner largely because Mom spares him the consequences of his own actions. Because his mom rescues him from being suspended from the school band, he does not have to worry much about the trombone. That is why he will continue "forgetting" And Mom will do the worrying for both.

This analysis serves to illustrate a major point: the key to understanding problematic behavior lies in the way in which child and parents interact with one another. A major focus of the behavioral-contextual analysis involves a determination of what a child discovers through his actions.

We ask the following:

What do his parents (and authority figures) typically do when he acts in problematic ways? Similarly, what do his parents do when he becomes emotional, when he acts out-of-sorts, angry, sad, or fearful? Regardless of a child's intentions, often the "purpose" of such behaviors is to exert some control over parental behavior. Generally speaking, much of a child's fearful, thoughtless, disruptive, and oppositional behavior can be best understood in terms of their effects on parental behavior.

REPLACING NEGATIVE WITH POSITIVE BEHAVIOR THROUGH NATURAL CONSEQUENCES

Although there is general agreement that families influence their children, how this is accomplished remains unclear. Yet, from a practical point of view it is most important to know how this influence proceeds. The approach discussed here emphasizes the role of consequences in the development of problematic behavior.

As mentioned previously, a "hidden" trove of natural consequences is already available at home. These consequences take place daily and repeatedly in the context of living and interacting with a child. These include consequences that benefit the child because they are fun, easy, and save him time and effort. Other consequences represent a cost to him because they are annoying, inconvenient, demand too much time, and require his focused effort.

The consequences are natural when they flow from the unique characteristics of the child's problematic behavior and the parent's typical efforts to manage it. The goal is to manage these natural consequences to motivate a child to switch from a problematic to a positive pattern of behavior.

Here are some of the special routines designed for parents of difficult children. Note that the child-parent reciprocal influence (discussed previously) lies at the heart of the behavioral solutions described here. Therefore, these routines were carried out largely at home by the parents involved. The following cases illustrate how the contextual-behavioral strategy may be implemented with a wide range of problematic behaviors.

Fearful Flora, a nine-year-old

The last time Flora was known to have slept in her own bed was when she was about five years old. Around that time, she shared her fears of being alone at night. As time went on she mentioned her fear along with just not feeling comfortable and safe in her room. Over the years when her parents encouraged her to sleep in her bedroom, Flora moaned, cried, and pleaded to sleep with her parents and stopped crying only when they finally allowed her to sleep with them. Flora welcomed this outcome, to be sure, but it also gave her parents a sense of relief and rest from all the crying and moaning.

For the last four years, Flora has slept every night with her parents. Mom and Dad tried everything to break the habit, using reasoning, buying new things for her room to make it more attractive and comfortable, offering rewards, and even veiled threats, which they never had the heart to act on. Over time, her parents were exhausted from having to share a bed with a growing child who twisted and turned through the night. When she was seven years old, Flora was taken to a professional therapist to help her overcome her fears and anxiety regarding sleeping in her room. Even after one year of therapy, however, Flora continued to sleep with her parents. Yet, Flora seemed unaware of her parents' depth of discomfort with the situation. She just loved sleeping with her parents. No wonder she resisted any efforts to take that experience away from her! On the other hand, her parents felt terribly conflicted. While they wanted their bed and privacy back, they also wanted to soothe their daughter. After all, their daughter mattered to them more than anything else in the world.

This is not such an unusual situation for a lot of parents. Think about it. How many times have you acquiesced to a sleepy child and allowed her to sleep with you? Ask yourself why you do it. You know why. You do it because you love your child, of course. You do it, even at the cost of your own needed rest. You would feel terribly guilty if you forced your child to spend the night in her bed while she cried and begged you to please let her sleep with you one more night! You would not want to reject a child's pleas and act unfeeling toward her. Instead, you want to be a good mom. So, you let her sleep with you, and your child quits crying and settles down for much-needed sleep. You have just solved the immediate problem. You have done right by your child and you feel good. Admittedly, it may be a short-term solution. The problem is that the next night the same routine and response is repeated. Unwittingly, Flora and her parents are in a circular reciprocal process of influencing one another.

Confronted with the same issue every night, Flora's parents resigned themselves to sleep three in one bed. An unintended consequence of this solution is that it locked them in a behavioral pattern that enabled Flora to enjoy a close, emotional, connection to her parents by insisting on sleeping with them. Because their influence over one another is reciprocal, the solution to the problem is to be found in the way they interact.

What was done to help Flora overcome her fear of sleeping alone?

After several years of sleeping with her parents, Flora seemed less interested than ever in sleeping in her own bed. The issue was how to disentangle Flora and her parents from a reciprocal pattern that kept them repeating the same cycle with the same negative outcome. Flora's parents agreed to try an alternative way to help their daughter become comfortable and secure sleeping in her own bed. Again, parents were coached to follow a different sleeping routine.

The first step was to strengthen Flora's emotional security before considering any change in her sleeping habits. To achieve this goal, we needed first to reframe the bedtime style of child-parent interaction and then arrange natural consequences attendant to sleeping with her parents. One afternoon, just home from school, Flora settled into her favorite activity, watching her cartoon programs on TV. During the commercial, mother explained to her that she and her father actually did not mind Flora sleeping with them every night. They were just tired of having to make the bed, and tidy up the bedroom by themselves every day. Since Flora used their bed every night, she needed to help in making the bed and straightening up the bedroom. Since Mom had not taught Flora how to make the bed and clean up the bedroom, she now had the time to teach her the chore. When Flora asked if Mom could teach her later after her TV program was over, Mom told her that this was the only time she had to show Flora how to do it. Besides, Mom reassured her that she could get back to her program as soon as she was finished with her chore. In the middle of making

Tip #5	To discourage unwanted behavior, collect a "user" fee that fits the context of the unwanted behavior.

up the bed and tidying the bed-room, Flora wanted to know if she had to do this work all the time. "No, Sweetie," responded her mother, "Only when you use our room and bed."

Takeaway # 12

Overprotecting a child tends to separate behaviors from their natural consequences.

Flora did not seem to enjoy the chore, as she would much rather be watching her shows on television uninterrupted. Still, Mom reassured her that after she got good at making the bed and straightening up the bedroom, she probably would not need to be shown how to do it every time. One afternoon, two afternoons, three afternoons, the mother interrupted Flora after she settled in to her TV programs, repeating that she needed help with the bedroom chores.

On the third night, at bedtime, Flora announced to her parents that she was very tired, and went upstairs to bed. However, instead of going into her parents' bedroom as was her usual routine, she went to bed in her own bedroom! Since she had not told her parents about it, they were not sure just what was going on. The next morning, she woke up in a good mood, and seemed pleased with herself. Her parents simply accepted this news and acted calmly about it. A few days later, Flora commented to her mother that she really liked her own bed much better than that of her parents. She has slept in her own bedroom ever since.

How did Flora overcome her fears?

Flora was a "clingy," anxious, fearful child who connected with her parents when her dependent behavior pattern evoked their protective nurturance. Therefore, the strategy employed here respected the way she connected with them by not changing her practice of sleeping with them. Rather, the strategy attached a natural consequence to her practice of sleeping with parents: she was to help with the next day's bedroom clean-up. She seemed to accept it as a fair request. An important component of this strategy was a daily training period in bed-making to coincide with Flora's leisure time. Mom asked her to leave whatever she was enjoying and to accompany her to their bedroom where she taught her how to make the bed. As soon as the training was over (5-8 minutes) Flora returned to her leisure activities. Her parents appeared satisfied with the new arrangement. However, after three days of cleaning and tidying up the parents' bedroom, Flora chose to sleep in her own bed. The next day she was no longer asked to help clean up her parents' bedroom. From that point on Flora stopped sleeping with her parents.

Although her parents expected Flora to show some signs of emotional distress, she did not show them. She was neither argumentative nor short-tempered following her change of behavior. Once Flora left her parents' bed, she behaved as if it was only natural for her to sleep in her bedroom. No special effort was made to discuss with Flora the merits of sleeping in her own bed, nor was there any special reward given to her on this account. However Flora no longer had a "free pass" to share her parents' bed. In a sense, a "user" fee was attached to sharing her parents' bed.

It took three days of practicing making the bed and tidying up her parents' bedroom for Flora to choose to abandon the bed she had been sharing with her parents for four years. What probably happened was that the experience of "paying" the "user fee" motivated Flora to review the benefits she received from sleeping with her parents and weighed the cost in effort, discomfort, and inconvenience involved in helping to clean and tidy up the parents' bedroom. Soon, she decided that the disadvantages of sleeping with her parents outweighed the advantages. Once she chose to sleep in her own bedroom, she did not return to sleep with her parents. The natural consequences attendant to each choice took over. She avoided having to clean up her parents' bedroom by choosing to sleep in and enjoy her own bed. Mom was very happy with Flora's showing "maturity," and thought that in time her daughter might also learn to make her own bed.

The constant help provided by parents to a "needy" child may unwittingly keep the problematic behavior going. Each child—Flora, Doreen, and Sammy—learned to connect with parents by behaving at the emotional level of children much younger than themselves.

The more Sammy's parents tried to assist him in getting what he pointed to, the more he depended on their help to get what he wanted. Yet, Sammy knew how to express verbally what he wanted. Similarly, Doreen's mother took on the responsibility of shielding her daughter from being late to school by driving her to school herself.

Flora's parents tried to help her get through her fears, by letting her sleep with them. However, the more they did so, the more important sleeping with them became to her.

Once again, an important characteristic of child-parent influence is that it is a reciprocal one. A child's behavior influences her parents' behavior just as much as they influence her own. Further, this reciprocal character of child-parent influence may even strain the marital relationship. This may be another unintended consequence stemming from parental reaction to a child's problematic behavior.

Good parents cannot help from protecting and soothing their children. This is only natural for parents to do. Overprotecting, however, has unintended results. Overprotecting a child teaches him to leave his worries at his parents' doorstep. Overprotecting him prevents him from learning how to deal with even a low level of frustration. So, what can you do? First, ask yourself if your child is misbehaving despite all your efforts to get him to quit. If so, you are ready to take the next step.

CHAPTER FIVE

A CHILD LEARNS THROUGH EXPERIENCES INVOLVING PERSONAL COST AND BENEFIT

Chances are, what you are doing right now to stop or change your child's behavior is, in fact, maintaining it. Consider that through all the missteps, challenges, and demanding behaviors, your child has gradually come to learn that you will cater to his every wish. Basically, your child expects that you will act as his chauffer, valet, full-time maid, spokesperson, and Memory Board. But, there is good news! Even though your child has

> **Takeaway #13**
>
> **Problematic behavior persists when personal benefits outweigh discomfort, and/or effort.**

learned to act as a dependent and helpless child, it is still possible for him to unlearn these patterns of behavior and learn to act in positive ways instead. But, how is a child going to unlearn his awful habits? I will tell you how. Briefly, to discourage a child from repeating problematic behavior, you need to alter your typical reaction to it.

Indeed, when parental efforts to help do not work, the perceived help may, in time, become the problem. Remember that Doreen's, Sammy's, and Flora's parents helped their own child give up negative behaviors and adopt positive

---

 Tip #6 | **To discourage unwanted behavior, amplify the natural inconveniences that fit the context of the uwanted behavior.**

---

ones. They achieved this goal by making sure that problematic behaviors resulted in inconvenience and added effort for the child rather than ease and comfort. For example, only when his pointing routine became a daily burden and a time-consuming effort to Sammy himself, did he quit pointing and choose to speak instead. In Flora's case, only when sleeping with her parents became a time-consuming and effortful chore to Flora herself, did she quit sleeping with her parents and choose to sleep in her own bedroom. Doreen now got up early in the morning, got dressed and ready for school, and caught the school bus–all this without any help from her mom. In effect, Doreen showed her teacher (as well as herself and her mother) that she was indeed a responsible student.

Sickly Simon, a seven-year-old

A seven-year-old boy, Simon, was brought for psychological consultation because of frequent stomach complaints. His mother was particularly concerned that he had missed six days in the last two weeks of school because he was not feeling well in the morning. After a medical examination, Simon's pediatrician referred him for psychological consultation because several medical tests revealed no organic basis for his complaints. Simon was an only child from a middle-class family. Mom was a stay-at-home mother and Dad was a hardworking man who left the house early in the morning and returned just in time for dinner.

Simon's case illustrates the contextual, functional approach favored here. The focus of evaluation was on examining the details of the child-mother interaction at home when he reported stomach pains. During the initial interview, the mother described how heart-wrenching it was for her to see Simon barely dragging himself doubled up in pain, complaining of a severe stomachache. To calm him down and help him feel better, she allowed her son to stay at home and miss school.

It was clear that her son's complaints affected her and that, naturally, she made every effort to soothe and comfort her son. To this end, when he complained about stomach pain and looked like he was having a bad morning, she allowed him to stay in bed and sleep late. Typically, by midmorning, Simon got up and watched TV or played with his Nintendo. Simon appreciated what his mother did for him but as he started to feel better, mother expected him to return to school. Within a few days of going to school, however, he again reported stomach pains, which, in turn, led Mom to keep him at home and to help him just as she had been doing all along.

Simon's mother came for a psychological consultation when her son was once again sick at home. Mom's description of Simon's physical complaints and her efforts to soothe and comfort him seemed to be linked in a way that promoted more complaints of stomachaches. Furthermore, his continuing complaints had a reciprocal influence on mother's assistance. The more Simon complained, the longer the time Mom spent soothing and assisting her son to feel better.

Simon's mother took her son's physical complaints seriously. Under these conditions, it would have been counterproductive (not to mention insensitive) to suggest that she ignore or minimize her son's complaints. Most loving parents would reject such advice, and rightly so. A caring parent would not turn her back on a child who has problems such as the ones reviewed here.

A special regimen was designed to help with Simon's stomach complaints. The strategy chosen here was to build an intervention based on the mom's own comfort zone in helping her son. Above all, she was encouraged to continue being a loving, sympathetic, and kind mom.

The relevant aspect of this get-well regimen centered on giving Simon an intensive TLC (tender loving care) experience within a structured virtual-hospital type of environment. Following the standard medical strategy, Mom

> **Takeaway #14**
>
> **Helplessness is learned, but can also be unlearned.**

told her son he needed three days of rest in bed and plenty of fluids. Food intake had to be regulated, because the symptom—stomachaches—suggested problems with his diet or possibly with his digestion. Therefore, meals were to be bland and more the type of hospital fare for convalescing patients. He was encouraged to drink lots of water or milk. No fast foods, cookies, or sweet snacks were allowed and chocolate milk nor soda drinks were allowed because of his condition. Therefore, Mom, like a nurse, took his meals in a tray to his bed. She checked on him ever so often but avoided talking about issues unrelated to his health. It was important that he got plenty of bed rest and that he avoid overexerting himself physically.

To help him get full rest, it was necessary to maintain quiet surroundings.

Age-appropriate reading books and school-related materials were made available in his room. A policy of no TV, computer games, and the like was followed during convalescence. Whenever he complained or asked his mother why he could not watch TV or eat potato chips, or play outside, she patiently explained to her son that she could not take a chance with his health, and that she would help him get through this difficult period until his health was restored.

The first day of this nursing care brought a mixed reaction from Simon. He liked being the focus of Mom's concern and not having to do anything or even talk about missing school. By the end of the day, however, he complained bitterly about having nothing to do. He was terribly bored, and he did not even have TV to pass the time! Mom empathized with him while adhering to the agreed-upon nursing care. When he asked how long he was supposed to stay in bed, Mom answered that it was difficult to say, but that often doctors recommended three days of bed rest and lots of fluids in cases like his.

By the second day, Simon was getting very annoyed and told his mother that he was feeling better and needed something good to eat. Mom reassured him by telling him that his appetite was a good sign, but that it would be best not to overdo eating. She prepared some pasta and served it to him in bed. Simon tried to persuade Mom that he really was feeling much, much better. Mom told him that she did not want him to rush and go back to school unless he really felt better. Finally, at his insistence, Mom agreed that if he continued to feel better by the next day he could leave his bed and have breakfast before he went to school. On the third day, he woke up bright eyed, smiling, and reassured Mom that he was not sick anymore. He ate all his breakfast, which was unusual for him, and then ran to catch the school bus. He no longer missed school nor did he complain of stomachaches or feeling ill.

On follow-up, a few months later, mother reported that Simon was no longer sickly but had become a happy and healthy child. He had friends in school and enjoyed playing soccer.

What was done to help Simon regain his health and well being?

Just as before, Simon was allowed to miss school when he was feeling sick and Mom took care of him at home. While Mom's usual tender, loving care continued, he found that the former personal benefits from being sick were absent: no more vacation type of stay at home for Simon. The "medical" type of treatment quickly became boring and rather inconvenient. As he got to feeling better and stronger, he really had to work hard to show Mom that he was ready to return to school. This time he chose health over sickness.

HOW TO DISCOURAGE PROBLEMATIC BEHAVIOR AND ENCOURAGE POSITIVE BEHAVIOR

Focusing on a child's misbehavior is not enough. We also need to know what the act of misbehaving does for him. Let us start with the general principle that when a child acts, he discovers what he does to his environment. In this manner, he learns that some things in his physical environment move and others do not when he pushes them. He also learns that sometimes his parents come quickly when he makes a lot of noise, when he cries, or when he misbehaves. Over time, he learns that some of the things he does are more likely than others to draw his parents' attention. Depending on the circumstances, he may learn that behaving appropriately does not do as much for him as behaving inappropriately. Therefore, when he misbehaves it is largely because misbehaving results in some personal benefit for him. A major part of his personal benefit comes from drawing parental attention and related personal benefits. Other times, it is because by misbehaving he reduces, avoids, or, postpones parental demands and expectations. In short, he tends to misbehave because of the personal cost/benefit consequences that follow his misbehavior.

Children nag, throw tantrums, withdraw, argue, ignore, and defy adults. Yet, their actions are not the result of planning and scheming. Children do not really choose to misbehave. Neither parents nor children are typically aware of the dynamics and meaning of a child's misbehavior because it takes place across time and situations that make it difficult to analyze and understand.

Take the example of Evan, a five-year-old, who cries, screams, and "pitches a fit" every morning just before breakfast. At such times he demands loudly that Dad tell

 Tip #7 | **To help you understand why a child misbehaves, notice what s/he gets out of acting in problematic ways.**

the adults, who are busy talking among themselves or helping with breakfast preparation, not to look at him when he comes down for breakfast. "I don't want them to look at me," he screams, and if someone does, he runs back to his room screaming all the way. To stop Evan from making an ugly scene at the top of the morning everyone in the family cooperates in doing the child's bidding.

Evan connects with Dad and the rest of the extended family through misbehaving. Should he stop his controlling routine, this connection would be broken. It is to Evan's benefit to continue to misbehave to maintain that connection.

Generally speaking, consequences may be subsumed under cost/benefit experiences. A child's interactions produce certain consequences that give him a personal cost-benefit experience. That is to say, sometimes what he does gives him joy, while other times, it causes him annoyance, and still other times what he does stimulates him or gives him the experience of control that energizes him to repeat his actions be they positive or negative.

Personal cost/benefit regulates a child's behavior.

Parents often wonder why a child who is loved and well cared for persists in being difficult. A child persists in being difficult because such style of interacting with his parents works to his advantage. Consequences that flow from acting in problematic ways favor him. Consequences are at the root cause of his behavior.

There are many variations on how a child may behave so as to "turn off" parental demands. A child may act needy, distant, forgetful, irritable, indifferent, defiant, and even aggressive with his parents. Despite the different forms that a child's problematic behavior may take, all of them have the same function or outcome: the behaviors postpone, prevent, or get rid of unwanted demands made of him. A child is likely to act in problematic ways when such actions bring him relief from boredom, frustration, and discomfort.

There are four major reasons that help explain why a child talks the talk but won't walk the walk.

1. A child learns the "talk" but not the "walk."

A child learns to neutralize and overcome parental control by telling parents what they want to hear. For example, a child may be reminded many times to put away his books, to turn off the TV, to stop his arguing, dawdling, and passive resistance. Often, he'll promise he will do just that, but these are just promises, promises, promises. Each time he makes a promise, he sounds so genuine that his parents cannot help but believe what he says. A difficult child, very good at the talking part, says what parents would like to hear. He may claim that he has done his schoolwork and his parents believe it and allow him to play computer games. The child's "talk" is so rewarding to parents that they in turn, are likely to award him some benefits.

2. "Talk the talk" is not the same as "walk the walk."

Say and do are two separate behavior patterns or skills that are often learned independently. A child may boast that he can ride a horse, but when faced with a horse, he may make excuses to avoid being near it. Such a child may have found that he gets a lot of attention whenever he claims to know how to ride a horse. No amount of talk, however, is going to substitute for the actual experience of riding a horse. That's because riding a real, live horse requires a special set of skills involving hands-on experience. Similarly, doing homework includes specific academic skills involving practice and hands-on experience. Over time, he only has to claim that he has done his work to discourage parental demands on his time. Generally, a problematic child is most likely to claim a variety of things that are simply not true, because it often takes parents a good deal of time and effort to verify such claims.

3. A child will not "walk the walk" because it's too much work!

A child will fail to "walk the walk," when it requires too much effort or work on his part. As it happens, there is often a real cost to a child for following his parents' requests and instructions. Typically, parental demands are likely to interrupt his preferred, fun activities to do something boring and "unnecessary" like cleaning his room, or

> **Takeaway #15**
>
> **When a child avoids tasks or situations s/he also gains control over a parent's behavior for related personal benefits.**

putting his stuff away. Clearly, from his point of view, there's little to gain by doing what his parents want him to do. Therefore, he is likely to turn a deaf ear to parental requests, or to promise but not do what he's promised.

4. A child can't "walk the walk" if he doesn't know how!

Sometimes, a difficult child does not follow through on his promises because he simply does not know how to do so. Indeed, in an effort to minimize stress and conflict, parents have already given up on making "real-world" demands on him. Under these circumstances, how is a child ever going to learn when he has never succeeded in "walking the walk"?

So, what's the problem?

Empty promises, then, may not necessarily reflect a child's laziness or deliberate refusal to do what he promised to do. Rather, they may reflect certain parental practices that shield him or rescue him from the "doing" part. The issue here is that a child's difficult behavior is not necessarily "the" problem. Rather, the parents' reaction to his lack of cooperation may have led them to gradually ask less of him. In time, as parents do for him what he is expected to do, he is prevented from learning to meet even minimal "real-world" demands.

Personal cost and benefit describe a child's experiences.

A child does not like and resists any efforts to limit or curtail his freedom to act. Limits and boundaries placed on him represent a cost he is not willing to bear. Doing household chores, helping with the yard, cleaning his room, and the like, are usually annoying and inconvenient. While these activities are neither humiliating nor painful, they take too much time, a good deal of effort, and compete with things he would rather do, such as playing outside, watching TV, or spending time on the computer. Doing what Mom or Dad wants imposes a personal cost to a child. As far as a child is concerned, complying with a parent's request exacts a personal cost. He is expected to stop, set aside what he likes to do, and, instead, work on very frustrating and terribly boring things. Part of the problem is that the time and effort involved doing chores not of his own choosing far outweigh the possible benefits to him. Of course, a child hates to spend his time that way, and it shows! Following instructions delivers very little if any benefit to a resistant child.

In short, behaving appropriately involves personal cost to a child: it requires a lot of effort, a lot of time, and a lot of trouble. From a child's point of view, he does not need that aggravation!

Here are two typical reasons why a child "dodges" instructions:

1. A child will avoid, delay, and postpone to do as instructed because what he is being asked to do interrupts his fun, requires too much work on his part, or both. Rather than getting into more trouble for disobedience, a child may give a socially more acceptable impression, that of a too distracted, forgetful, less energetic, and even lazy child. In all events, a child will avoid the cost involved in

doing things that do not immediately favor him.

2. Boredom is an experience a child will escape from and avoid altogether. Lack of stimulation or cessation of stimulation are felt as boring and affect how he feels and how he deals with his parents. The experience of boredom is costly to him as wasted time that he could have spent doing fun things instead of feeling pushed to lose his cool.

Generally, a child enjoys experiences involving creative efforts, sports, and school-related activities that foster and maintain a strong connection to parents and peers. Additional personal benefits may include spending time with friends, gaining access to computer games, cell phone, watching TV, and purchasing CDs, DVDs, and related electronic devices. Typically, a child spends time engaged in these various activities because they have intrinsic value, are fun, and offer lots of opportunities to make friends.

There is another and most important subset of personal benefits that might be regarded as individual, subtle, and idiosyncratic. Among these are comfort, convenience, ease of access to and from a variety of situations, and often being the focus of attention deserving special consideration.

Takeaway #16

Rescuing a child from frequent self-produced discomfort further encourages the child to repeat the behavior.

Child-parent interactions yield personal cost-benefits.

Setting aside for a moment a child's need for safety and parental love, most child-parent interactions center around a child's request or demand for attention and self-oriented benefits. Typically, a parent adjusts to a child's needs and wants while maintaining a modicum of control. The world of a child is largely dependent on close relationships with parents and significant others. It is through frequent interactions with parents, or significant others, that a child learns about his world and about himself. It is also through close interaction with a child that a parent learns about a child's internal world and about his sense of self-esteem.

As a child discovers that there are personal costs and benefits to behaving well or poorly, he will tend to repeat behaviors that favor him and avoid those that require much effort on his part. Subtle benefits include being excused from disobeying, or behaving poorly, and being granted favors and benefits in advance of meeting a wide range of parental rules and social expectations. Most of these personal cost/benefit experiences are made possible by parents and significant others through close and frequent interaction with a child.

Good behavior has a cost . . .

Behaving well often takes the form of polite manners and respectful behavior toward parents and family members. Some children seem oblivious to the social amenities and courtesies valued by their own families. This is mortifying to parents because a child's uncouth or gross behavior reflects poorly on their efforts to teach him to behave appropriately. Still, while many children do behave well, behaving well does not come easy to them. From a child's perspective, good behavior is often not worth the effort. Indeed, good behavior requires a child to take valuable time away from doing cool things. Besides, good behavior is often boring and not much fun.

. . . but a child learns to "cut" costs.

To reduce the amount of effort, time, and boredom involved in behaving well, a child will try three major ways to comply with Mom's instructions and expectations without actually succeeding.

1. Often, he will act distracted or forgetful, and will claim to have misunderstood his parents' instructions. When asked if he has done his homework, he may reassure his mom that he will do it right after supper, and then of course not do it.

2. At other times, he will complain of feeling poorly, argue, become emotional, defiant, and refuse to listen to reason.

3. Now and then he will actually start to do what he was asked, but will do so slowly, slovenly, and put the least effort into the task.

Tip #8	To prompt behavior, introduce "heads-up" information to "pull" the appropriate behavior from a child's repertoire.

Over time these behaviors will go from annoying to confrontational so that parents may lose their temper and self-control. Parents may shout, scream, and order a child to stop misbehaving or threaten him with time-out, loss of TV, and other privileges: often without success. Finally, a parent is likely to offer a generous modification of what was expected of a child including a reduction, suspension, and even cancellation of the parents' original request in exchange for minimal compliance.

It is through a process like this that a child's style of interacting with parents develops as it serves him to influence and modify parental rules to his satisfaction.

Adorable Adam, a five-year-old

Adam is an adorable little boy who charmed his teachers in kindergarten with his intelligence and verbal skills. Teachers found him delightful but too talkative and easily distracted. At home, however, Adam complained about school. He reported to his mom that every day they were doing the same thing, the same activity every time. He seemed bored with what was going on in the classroom. On the other hand, Adam's parents' major concern was about his behavior at home. Adam, an only child, needed a lot of help from his mom. Every day, Mom had to dress him in the morning or he would not get dressed in time to go to school. At night, he needed help to get undressed and into his pajamas to go to bed. He refused to eat unless Mom spoon-fed him at breakfast and also at dinnertime. Mom had tried talking to him at length, but no amount of persuasion or rewards worked. Whenever Mom tried to stop the spoon-feeding, Adam refused to eat. According to his mom, this had been going on since he was a baby. Surprisingly, at school, he did better. He ate his lunch along with his peers. No one would ever guess he had to be spoon-fed to eat at home. Adam's infant-like behavior compelled his parents to take care of him as if he were a baby. Because of his helpless behavior, one might infer that Adam was just not quite ready to say goodbye to his babyhood!

Jump-start the desired behavior.

One evening before bedtime, Mom informed Adam that she had watched a TV program showing what five-year-old children could do. She shared her amazement: she did not know how many things five-year-olds could do. She thought it would help her to remember what five-year-old children are able to do by attaching the list on the refrigerator door. She then read the list aloud to him:

1. In the morning, gets ready for school: dresses and puts shoes on.

2. In the evening, gets ready to go to bed: undresses and puts pajamas on.

3. Eats breakfast and dinner by himself without any help.

Adam just listened to his mom as she read the list, but asked no questions nor showed any special reaction to this information. The next day, Adam got up when his mother woke him, dressed, put on his shoes, and ate his breakfast. This was the first time he ever did these four things by himself. Previously, he had to be awakened several times, dressed, helped with his shoes, and escorted to breakfast. More startling was that, instead of waiting for the usual spoon-feeding from Mom, he ate breakfast on his own. However, that evening, Adam refused to eat until Mom spoon-fed him.

Starting the second day, he again got up, dressed, put on his shoes, went down to the kitchen, and ate breakfast on his own. That evening, he ate dinner on his own. At bedtime he got ready for bed, undressed, put on his pajamas, and went to bed without any trouble. Adam continued to do well, and has also become responsible in other areas. He no longer relies on his parents to do what he can do for himself. No more arguments or entreaties were necessary for him to quit his age-inappropriate dependence on his mom to wait on him hand and foot.

What was done to help Adam use the skills he already had?

To understand how the change in Adam's behavior came about, we must remember that he was highly verbal and doing well in school. In fact, on several occasions he had already complained to Mom that the teacher was teaching material that he already knew, that he had already done before, and that was boring for him to do again. In a sense he seemed to have seen himself as smarter than and perhaps ahead of his classmates. He knew he had the skills already. He did not need to learn anything new. Indeed, he already ate unassisted at school. He also knew how to dress himself. So, why did he need so much help? It is likely that, emotionally, Adam felt good, and more connected to Mom, by acting "needy." Indeed, the family's full attention and assistance was lovingly provided when he was helpless. He was comfortable that way. It worked well for him and he had no interest in giving that up.

Finding out about the list of abilities of a five-year-old seemed to have functioned as a "yardstick" that Adam could compare his own skills against. He could compare his smartness in school ("very good") to his smartness at home ("not so good"). If he was as smart as he thought he was, how come he was not able to do the things that five-year-olds do at home?

Once Adam found out that he did not measure up against what children his age do, he became motivated to show Mom and himself that he could match what five-year- olds do. Adam's major goal and reward was to show Mom he was a smart five-year-old boy, not just in school, but also at home! What seemed to have triggered Adam's behavior change was the information regarding the capabilities of five-year-olds. He was not taught any new skill, nor were there any special rewards given to him for stopping his previous dependent style of behavior. It might be said that Adam's behavior illustrates a very real instance of "learned helplessness" acquired and maintained through personal benefits provided by his loving and somewhat overindulgent parents at home.

The strategy up to now has been on changing the consequences that encourage misbehavior so as to allow an alternative positive behavior to replace it. A complementary strategy is to work with the antecedents (or cues) to behavior.

Clearly, a shortcut is to engage a child so as to make contact with his likes and dislikes, dreams and fears. We then invite the child through these cues to "look" within himself and to choose to act, guided by beliefs and skills that offset or displace misbehavior. In the context of child-parent inter-actions, it is the unexpressed beliefs, and concerns of a child that often trigger new behavior. The "heads up" procedure derives from such a strategy and was employed in Adam's case, and also in the following one.

Harrison, nine-years-old, is the only child of a single, loving mom. Divorced, she often felt that she needed to be both a mother and a father to her son. Soon after her divorce, Harrison, at age four, started coming to his mom's bed because he was afraid of sleeping alone. Mom thought it was only natural for him to need her reassurance and love. Over time, however, he was unwilling to return to his bed. Admittedly, at different times, Mom tried various ways to encourage him to sleep in his bed, but she had little success. Mom did not want him to feel rejected, so she resigned herself to ac-cepting his need to sleep in her bed. Finally, after five years of waiting for Harrison to quit sleeping with her, she sought professional help. She was "at the end of her rope."

Harrison was a highly verbal boy with bright eyes, a win-ning smile and a sense of humor. After gaining his confi-dence and getting to know his daily routine, I compli-mented him on his schoolwork and his efforts to help his mom at night. It took a few sessions to talk about his mom who came home exhausted from work and needed a well-deserved rest. Yet, Mom was not a very good sleeper. De-spite all his help, she still did not sleep well. Clearly, she needed his help. I just wondered how much longer he had to help her this way. After all, Mom was almost thirty years-old! Perhaps, he could help her learn to sleep by herself in a gradual way so that she would feel comfortable about it. Maybe it was worth a try. Besides, he could always join her if she seemed to be having a hard time sleeping alone.

Within two weeks, Mom called to ask excitedly what I had told her son. I, in turn, asked what all the excitement was about. She then told me that Harrison was now sleeping in his bed, and had told her to call him if she needed him!

How did Harrison quit sleeping with his mom?

Sleeping together was something they did as an expression of mutual love and emotional support. However, Mom thought her son was too old to continue sleeping with her. But what if there was another interpretation of the same event? What if Harrison did not know how to disengage from his mom without making her feel bad? Which of these interpretations is true? The question is somewhat like, Is a glass of water half empty or half full? It depends. Maybe both are true. By reframing their sleeping together as a situation where Mom was the one who was being helped by her son, he was encouraged to do some thinking to find an alternative way of helping her sleep. In time, when he went to sleep in his own bed, he felt he had encouraged Mom to gradually get used to sleeping on her own.

A marvelous illustration of the usefulness of the "heads up" rule is the following news report that came in the late 1990s (www.snopes.com/risque/juvenile/lipstick.asp).

A certain private school in Washington was recently faced with a unique problem. A number of twelve-year-old girls had begun to use lipstick and would apply it in the bathroom. Then they would press their lips to the mirror leaving dozens of little lip prints. Every night the maintenance man removed the prints, but the next day the girls would put them back. Finally, the principal called all the girls to the bathroom where she explained that these lip prints were causing a major problem for the custodian who had to clean the mirrors every night. (You can just imagine the yawns from the little princesses.) To demonstrate how difficult it was to clean the mirrors, she asked the maintenance man to show the girls how much effort was required. He took out a long-handled squeegee, dipped it in the toilet, and cleaned the mirror with it. Since then, there have been no lip prints on the mirror.

The girls were not taught any new skill, nor were there any special rewards given to the girls for cooperating with the custodian. All that was needed to have the girls stop pressing their lipsticked lips on the mirror was to familiarize the girls to the custodian's cleaning method. This prompted immediate self-control on the part of the little princesses.

CHAPTER SIX

PARENTS ARE MANAGERS OF CONSEQUENCES

Parents are often pushed to react to a child's misbehavior with little or no time to reflect on it. Sometimes, they vacillate between letting a child experience the consequences of his actions and protecting him from them.

Hot-tempered Hanna, an eight-year-old

Hanna and Mom were shopping at the supermarket. As they were leaving the store, Mom noticed that Hanna was carrying a little toy bunny.

Mom: (Suspicious) Have you paid for that?
Hanna: (Acting offended) No, Mom, I thought you did!
Mom: (Annoyed) I didn't even know you had picked it up. Go and take it back!
Hanna: (Aggressive and screaming) But I don't want to do that, Mom. I'm not going to do it. You take it back!

Assume you walked past this scene in the supermarket and did not see how it ended. Now, who do you think should take the stolen item back to the store, Hanna or her loving mother? Ask yourself, What kind of lesson does Mother wish Hanna to learn from this incident?

It may help to list a few of Mom's possible choices:

1. "Hanna, I'll take it back myself but I don't ever want you to do that again."

2. "You take it back Hanna, and explain that you thought I had paid for it."

3. "You're going to take it back, and I will go with you."

By selecting #1, Mom is shielding her daughter from experiencing the natural consequences of her own action. As Hanna is neither inconvenienced nor made responsible for her action she is likely to behave in a similar way in the future.

By selecting #2, Mom is allowing her daughter to face a natural consequence that flows from Hanna's own action. Hanna will be both inconvenienced, annoyed, embarrassed, and made responsible for taking the toy. Hanna is likely to avoid a similar behavior in the future.

By selecting #3, Mom is softening the natural consequences of Hanna's action while still holding her responsible. This choice is a compromise between being rescued from facing the natural consequences of her action to being exposed to some of these consequences. This last choice allows Mom to incrementally expose her daughter to the natural consequences of her own action.

As it happened, Hanna's mother selected choice #1. She did so to avoid having an ugly scene in public. Here, the likely lesson for Hanna is that she does not have to worry when she gets into trouble. Mom will rescue her and take care of her when things get rough or difficult.

Parents typically manage the consequences attendant to a child's behavior. They often select what, in their judgment, is the appropriate learning experience for a challenging child. Sometimes, this brings unanticipated results.

As was discussed earlier, a "needy" child often "chooses" to behave in a somewhat extreme, and dramatic, way because such behavior compels parents to refocus their attention and concern on him.

POSITIVE PARENTING AND OFF-BEAT COMMUNICATION: TOOLBOX TO DETOUR, REDIRECT, AND RECALIBRATE COMMUNICATION

Children with problematic behavior are so used to their parents' style of management that they do not expect them to change the way they talk, think, or react. Rather, children expect their parents to remain the same as they know them. This helps explain why children are ill-prepared to know how to deal with a parent whose style of interaction is no longer predictable. Therefore, in order to bring about change, parents need to explore a new style of interacting with an overly dependent and demanding child. The goal of this new style of dealing with a difficult child is to interrupt the repetitive and negative cycle of interaction to create a new context for positive interactions.

Imagine a couple dancing a well-rehearsed, almost choreographed dance (waltz or tango) in which each dancer anticipates the other's moves and thereby keeps the dance going. Now, imagine that from time to time one of the dancers tries out an unrehearsed "dance step" that throws the dancing partner off his timing and routine. It would not take long before the afflicted dancing partner decided to quit dancing. Now, consider a child-mother interaction as a smooth, well-practiced, "dance" where, from time to time, Mom inserts a new "dance step" that will interrupt and confuse a child, who will not know how to resume the "dance." A child becomes confused when faced with an unfamiliar, "dance step" in the old "choreographed" child-parent interaction. Finding it difficult to "read" his parents' behavior serves to motivate a child to find alternative ways of connecting with them. The net outcome from causing such an interruption is that it gives you and the child a chance to move away from the repetitive and negative cycle that makes everyone miserable.

DEVELOPING RESILIENCE

Most of the time, a problematic child is somewhat slow and resistant to comply with instructions and to observe limits imposed by parents or teachers. Often, he may feel stress and tension returning home from school. He may express dissatisfaction with the teacher and the school. He may complain that school is boring. He may overreact or act in a demanding, impulsive, impatient, and generally disagreeable manner. At home, he is used to doing things his way, at his own pace, and expects that his teacher, and others, will adapt to his needs and expectations rather than the other way around. As he has long been protected from experiencing frustration, he is easily overwhelmed when things do not go his way. He loses his cool and does not know how to compose himself and start anew. To make things worse, he rejects any efforts to calm him down and help him. Understandably, he is frustrated and does not know how to react to failure.

At this point, it is too late to expect such a child to tough it out. True, he needs to get over his frustration and anger, but a sink-or-swim approach is often counterproductive. An alternative approach is favored here. Admittedly, he needs to develop a new pattern of behavior that protects him from getting easily confused and upset when things are not going his way.

The goal for a child is to gradually learn to become resilient. Resilience is an acquired skill that helps a child bounce back from feeling down, unappreciated, or misunderstood. To achieve this goal it will be necessary to give a child a variety of experiences at home that have one major feature in common: they all slow down his pace and manner of interacting with parents. Specifically, the strategy is to gradually expose a child to frustration in "baby doses" that are typically encountered at home such as when he cannot have his own way, or is being asked to help with chores. This strategy allows a child to feel and go through the beginning, middle, and end of a frustrating episode, and also experience growing success in controlling his emotional response to it.

A child's resilience is built not by shielding him from natural inconveniences and mild disappointments encountered in daily living but by allowing him to gradually learn to cope with such experiences.

Communication problems are the effects, not causes, of misbehavior.

Misbehavior is sometimes viewed as a primitive form of communication. Presumably, once communication is established, problematic behavior will be resolved.

Strategic parenting turns this upside down: communication problems are the effects, not the causes, of misbehavior. A child misbehaves because of the personal benefits he gains by misbehaving. How does that happen? Remember, it is parents who in reaction to misbehavior provide consequences that fuel it. Therefore, we can resolve communication problems by changing the parents' reaction to misbehavior. That is how parents can help a child quit unwanted behaviors.

TOWARD EFFECTIVE COMMUNICATION: DO'S AND DON'T'S

To shift communication from disruptive and confrontational to calming and helpful requires the following strategy:

1. Rather than accuse or blame the child, the strategy is to have the child hear Mom (or Dad) blame themselves for the unwanted behavior. By so doing a child is no longer on the defensive and quickly relaxes his otherwise argumentative and somewhat aggressive stance.

2. Cultivate a little ditzy, somewhat forgetful, lax kind of parenting to replace the typical overindulgent parenting style.

3. Slow down and stop trying to do everything to please your demanding, high-maintenance child. The chances are you already work outside your home and, in addition, take care of the family meals, chores, and help your child in countless ways.

4. You want to act less efficient, more "natural," and less driven.

5. Cultivate taking care of your own immediate priorities. Your child will not learn to respect your own time constraints if you do not do that yourself.

6. Whenever your child demands or requires your immediate attention and assistance, be calm, loving, and say something like, "Be with you in a minute, darling." Then, give him the experience of waiting for one to three minutes before you finish your own activities. Remember, you will still be able to help him get what he wants but it will take a bit more time than usual. Soon, he will feel more motivated to cut short his waiting for you and, instead, take care of his own needs.

By doing these things, you are building your child's resilience to the natural inconveniences, and mild discomfort involving school-related assignments as well as daily expectations at home. This will help him adapt to typical situations where he is expected to wait or to start or stop action on a teacher's request or your own request. Over time he will deal much more effectively with not getting his way.

GUIDELINES FOR ANGER MANAGEMENT

Generally speaking, most verbal exchanges between child and parent are rapid, emotionally laden, and do not allow a parent time to think of an appropriate response or reaction to a child's challenge. Here are some guidelines to minimize escalation of emotional exchanges by child and parent. A major feature of these guidelines is to introduce a variety of non-verbal "street bumps" that slow, delay, and, in time, detour a child's behavioral momentum away from his usual path to anger and misbehavior. In so doing, these moves promote the development of resilience and self-control.

QUICK VERBAL AND NON-VERBAL "MOVES"

Do the following when a child is getting angry and upset:

1. Drastically reduce stimulation (no arguing, no yelling, no rehashing of the past).

2. Minimize eye contact (no accusative glares).

3. Speak in a low, soft, kind voice; slow your speech (no speed talking, no third-degree interrogatory).

4. Move slowly, offer physical guidance (no grabbing, pushing, pulling).

5. Focus on listening for feelings and thoughts (no orders, no commands).

6. Now and then nod your head, indicating you are with him (no rush to establish blame).

7. Remain calm, and pretend you are not hearing the anger behind his demands. You are dealing with a difficult but loved person in your home. Do not take his attitude personally.

8. Use voice-control. Otherwise, your tone, speed, and intensity may convey anger, insult, or sarcasm and trigger negative behavior.

9. Avoid nagging "reminders" as they function as "fighting" words. Instead use few words: "dishes," "homework," "dog."

10. Do not bring up past transgressions once a child has shifted from negative to positive behavior.

11. Do not give him suggestions to improve his behavior while still in the middle of an emotional episode. A child will perceive your suggestions either as orders or as ultimatums. Either way he will resist and go against you.

12. Cultivate an amiable and easy demeanor.

Setting limits and boundaries will most likely produce emotional reaction from children unaccustomed to them. Change is seldom celebrated by somewhat spoiled, controlling children.

Avoid giving directives: give choices instead.

Make an announcement, or advance an alert, that prompts a child to consider behaving in a way that makes him feel he is the one deciding what he is going to do. You are not pressuring him to do something he has never done before. Rather, you are letting him know that there are at least two to three options for him to choose from. You want to present the options so that each has advantages and disadvantages. You should not tell him what option you would like him to choose. If you do that he has to contradict you and choose to continue to misbehave. Why would he do that? Frequently, a difficult child wants to show his parents that he is the boss, and one way to establish this is by rejecting parental advice or choices. If you suggest that he select A and not B he is most likely to reject your suggestion and instead select B. That is why you must resist telling him what he should choose. It is best if you leave it to him to choose the option that is most beneficial or favorable and least costly and inconvenient to him. Favorable may mean to him that what he chooses shows he is cool, sharp, smart, aware, and in control of himself. Inconvenient may mean to him that the option involves too much work, effort, or a boring and endless hurry-up-and-wait runaround. The choice is his. Admittedly, you give him only the options that you can also live with.

A child feels his way through action.

It is important to remember that a child is not looking at a situation from his parents' point of view. Generally, he does

 Tip #9 | **To discourage the start of unwanted behavior, stay calm, look away, and act busy, but show interest when the child switches to appropriate behavior.**

not think or plan inappropriate actions in advance. Rather, he simply acts by feel. As his parents adjust to his misbehavior, he will tend to repeat it as that makes him feel connected to his family and comfortable within himself.

"American Idol" Arthur, a six-year-old

Arthur imitates Grandma's slurred speech and laughs at her. His parents think it's cute at first, but then smile at him and, in a matter-of-fact voice, tell him, "That is enough, Honey," but Arthur keeps imitating Grandma. Although his parents told him to stop, their non-verbal, body language told him they were also entertained by his performance. Admittedly, his parents had asked him in no uncertain terms to quit making fun of Grandma, but no matter how often he was reminded to stop, he continued with his "act." His parents wondered why he persisted in annoying his poor grandmother.

What was done to help Arthur become sensitive to other people's feelings?

Arthur gravitates to his "act" because "good" behavior does not get him as much attention from his audience. He likes entertaining his parents, and imitating his grandmother is just part of his "act." His parents cannot help to react as they do when he does his impersonations of Grandma. In one sense, Arthur has not learned an alternative way to interest and hold the attention of his audience. As there is no cost, no downside to his misbehavior, he tends to continue with his "act."

Arthur's parents needed to give him a special experience to

change his annoying behavior toward Grandma. One evening after supper, he started his usual "impersonation" of Grandmother. This time, instead of smiling or watching the act, his parents looked at the ceiling or the floor, kind of lost in thought. As he continued, he asked them to watch him. They did not answer but simply appeared thoughtful.

Arthur, somewhat anxiously asked, "Aren't you gonna watch me Dad?"

Dad replied, "We've seen that show before. Do you know any other show that we could watch? You don't? That's too bad. Well, we might as well get ready for bed. So get your pajamas on."

Why does a child act "needy" or act out when he knows better?

Arthur tried the same act for several more days, and was visibly irritated as his parents simply paid no attention to his act and made no sign that suggested they were interested in it. When he asked why they didn't watch his act, they pointed out that they had seen that act before but wondered if he had a new act. It took a few more days, and Arthur surprised them with a new act. This time he imitated the sounds of the coyote cartoon and of Sylvester the Cat. His parents watched the show and expressed their delight with the way the cat spoke. "That was not easy," they said and Arthur agreed he was going to do more sounds. In time even Grandma could join in the audience and enjoy the new act. In his search for an audience Arthur finally connected positively with his family!

A frequent approach to stopping misbehavior is to order a child to stop it and to spend some time discussing the error of his ways. Often parents are so very worried about harming a child's self-esteem that they simply talk and talk and talk some more before they finally get a child to promise he will not misbehave again. However, this did not work with Arthur. One possibility was that all the fuss provoked by his misbehavior functioned as a shortcut for Arthur to connect to his parents. To offer Arthur an opportunity to connect differently with his parents, they stopped telling him how to behave. Instead, they withdrew the attention that his misbehavior commanded. This made it easier for Arthur to experience the consequences of his choices: he "lost" his audience when he misbehaved, but regained it when he behaved appropriately. Soon, he came back with another "act" and was able to reconnect with his family at a positive emotional level.

PROBLEMATIC BEHAVIOR AND
SOCIAL CONNECTEDNESS

Before you can take corrective measures, consider the possibility that the situation in which a difficult child finds himself makes him most vulnerable to acting "needy," dependent, or acting out. This means that certain events either at home, school, or in the playground are likely the causes of a child's conflict and stress. In a sense, a child's somewhat dramatic behavior is opportunistic. It emerges as a "solution" that provides him relief from stress. In the medical area, one talks about certain illnesses or infections as being opportunistic in that they most likely occur when the suppressed immunological system of an individual and the surrounding environmental conditions interact in such a way as to produce illness.

In a similar way, dramatic behavior is most likely to occur when a child's needs, or vulnerabilities, and the demands of the situation interact so as to produce it. For example, a shy and somewhat fearful child may overreact emotionally if the social context demands his active participation. Similarly, a child of a contested and acrimonious divorce may act in a confusing manner

Takeaway #17

A high-need child is rarely satisfied with the attention he gets and will seek even negative attention.

because his parents often expect him to demonstrate love or loyalty to one parent over the other. Under these circumstances, a child is bound to think that he will disappoint one parent or the other and feel guilty no matter what he does. Therefore, it may be useful to view a child's unusual behavior as reacting to the multiple social contexts that influence ongoing parental issues and interactions affecting him.

A "difficult" child has unmet nurturance needs. Misbehavior from such a child is most likely to take on an exaggerated or dramatic form because it is most likely to

1. be overlooked, condoned, and excused;

2. result in parental attention, and acknowledgement;

3. gain access to something he likes or wants (such as an electronic game, playing outdoors, television);

4. lead to some concession for him to stop his negative behavior, such as "I'll drive you to play with Timmy if you stop banging the door;"

5. help him get rid of annoying parental demands in general.

These various types of consequences have the opposite effect of what parents want: they reward a child's dramatic misbehavior and make it more likely to be repeated. How is that possible? The previous cases, including Silent Sammy, Fearful Flora, Dreamy Doreen, and American Idol Arthur, illustrate a child's "discovery" of the personal, emotional benefit to be gained through inappropriate behavior. In short, he benefits from making such "choices." This is a process that is not easy for parents to see. Parents believe that a difficult child simply does not know he is making poor choices. That explains why parents spend an enormous amount of time trying to reason and persuade a child to see the error of his ways. As discussed above, it is not that he does not know the difference. Rather, it is that the "poor" choices actually benefit him.

Children "read" parents like a book.

The children described in these examples are different in many ways, but they have one thing in common. These children have spent a good deal of time repeating their respective problem behaviors and provoking a predictable reaction from their parents. Sometimes, parents are already sensitive to their child's early medical issues that might include a child's premature birth, some unusual illnesses, delay in achieving early childhood developmental benchmarks, and the like. In an effort to make up for perceived deficiencies, parents lovingly do the best they can to reassure a child, sometimes to the point of overindulging him. Unwittingly, this often sets up a pattern of child-parent interaction in which a child reverts to earlier patterns of behavior in which he replays an immature and dependent role that evokes parents' concerted efforts to soothe and nurture him.

Over time children learn to "read" their parents like a book in that they know exactly how parents will react to whatever they do or say. This explains why parent-child heated arguments and struggles have an air of being choreographed. Both child and parent, learn to anticipate the "dance steps" that each will take and escalate their emotional reaction to end in the same familiar impasse. All the same, parents will feel helpless to prevent these emotionally charged confrontations.

Angelina was a cute, seven-year-old little girl who was never pleased with anything her parents did for her. She demanded and her parents provided her with the specific toys, clothing, DVDs, and other items she wanted to have, but once she had them, it did not take long before she lost interest in them. She then resumed her search for new and more stimulating things to buy. All the while, her parents tried to tell her that it was a waste of money to keep getting things for her that did not make her happy. They told her they could save this money for a vacation for the family, or perhaps buy something that really was needed at home. They tried to reason with her about how things do not make people happy, but to no avail. That kind of talk seemed to infuriate and upset her. She demanded that they buy what she "needed" and was so emotionally upset that her parents thought it would be less stressful for all to just buy her things. When they did so, Angelina no longer was upset or frustrated, at least for a short while.

A "needy" child and a parent influence one another.

Because the major source of motivation for a child is social, a child likes to be the center of attention. A child wants to be listened to, acknowledged, accepted, and appreciated by his parents. Parents are a child's basic audience and "support group." Often, a child wants to impress his parents by showing off his growing skills. We have all seen a child jump into a pool hundreds of times and ask his parents, over and over, to watch him while he does so.

We have also seen and heard a child cry at bedtime. This often leads to intense, emotional interaction with Mom, as she attempts to reassure her child that she loves her but that she really has to go to bed because it's past her bedtime. Eventually, a child's crying evolves into expressions of fear and requests to stay up or be allowed to sleep with parents. As a child continues to cry, Mom promises she will read to her if she quits crying and goes to bed. In time, a child learns to cry to have Mom read to her. These circumstances often lead a child and parent to repeat the same cycle of reciprocal influence, both emotional and behavioral. These are common experiences that illustrate the ease with which a child and parent influence one another. The medium of influence is their style of interaction with one another.

Typically, misbehavior forces a shift in the emphasis and

order of priorities of the family's concerns. In effect, Mother may focus her attention more on her "needy" child than on the rest of her family. Soon, this may trigger some conflict in the married couple, not to mention the siblings. If parents are in disagreement about how to deal with a child's problematic behavior, a child will act so as to split his parents by siding with whomever is more "understanding" of his problem, and more likely to grant him favors. One may view such a process as a way for a child to emotionally connect to his parents.

Sometimes, problematic behavior creates emotional turmoil in the family and may result in overparenting and rescuing a child from self-produced stress and frustration. A problematic child seeks such an interaction because it stimulates, energizes, and serves to connect him to his parents. These are some of the personal benefits a child gains when he misbehaves. Over time, this also allows him to experience a vague sense of influence and control over his parents' behavior.

Firebug Bugsy, a nine-year-old

Bugsy was the nice-looking son of a middle-class married couple. He was a friendly and rather playful boy. He was a good student and generally a well-behaved child. Bugsy had been caught playing with matches in the past and Dad explained to him the dangers involved. Sometimes Mom sat with Bugsy, and spent a good deal of time to explain to him the importance of not playing with matches. Bugsy was apologetic and seemed to understand the importance of safety for the house and the family. Still, he could not be trusted, and his parents could not relax. What they did was to remind him every day to make sure he did not get any ideas related to playing with matches.

Sometime later, however, his family was shocked when part of the kitchen caught on fire, and they had to call the Fire Department. It happened early in the afternoon. Mom was somewhere in the house, and Dad was at work. The only other person at home was Bugsy. Fortunately, the damage was moderate and no one was hurt. Initially, he denied any connection to the fire. After some discussion, however, he told his parents that it was an accident. He was just striking a few matches and throwing them in a wastebasket and watching them burn, but suddenly something in the wastebasket caught fire and it spread to a small section of the kitchen. His parents were upset with him but they also felt grateful that he was not hurt.

At that time, he was again given clear and firm instructions to stop his dangerous play with matches. "We tell him that what he is doing is wrong and dangerous, that it is very upsetting, and that we won't put up with it anymore. We take away his privileges, TV, computer, and other things. We take things away sometimes for a week or more," they explained.

Still, these efforts had little or no effect because a few weeks later, a fire started in Bugsy's room and Mom called the Fire

Tip #10 | **To discourage inappropriate and encourage appropriate behavior instead, set a time and place to practice the appropriate behavior or skill during a time that conflicts with a child's preferred activities.**

133

Department. Bugsy and Mom were at home, and again the fire seemed to have happened accidentally. Apparently, Bugsy was just playing with a few matches when the window drapes in his room caught fire and blackened the wall of the room before Mom was able to put it out. This second fire was the basis for Bugsy's parents to take him to a psychologist.

What was done to help Bugsy quit playing with fire?

A major change consisted in re-interpreting for Bugsy his failure to stop playing with matches. Basically, it was not all his fault. His own "accidents" when lighting matches indicated that he really did not know how to control a fire. Clearly, he had not been properly taught fire safety. What was needed was to discontinue the emphasis on verbal instructions alone and to include hands-on training involving fire-safety procedures. This approach relieved Bugsy from having to insist that what had happened was an accident. He was also receptive to listen to his parents describe the details of fire-safety training. Bugsy did not argue with his parents regarding the importance of wearing the appropriate protective clothing during training. The protective clothing included a fire-retardant apron, safety gloves, and a sturdy cap selected for this purpose.

In addition, he was shown a set of items relevant to fire-drill training that were stored in the carport. The training set included the following:

1. A standing barbeque grill

2. A bag of kitty litter

3. A fire-retardant apron

4. Safety gloves

5. A sturdy cap

6. A box of safety matches

7. A water can filled with water

The training was comprised of several steps:

1. Bugsy collected the seven items described above from the storage area in the carport and arranged the grill in an open area of the yard designated for this purpose. This included putting kitty litter on the base of the grill and placing a filled water can on the ground next to the grill.

2. He wore the appropriate clothing: a fire-retardant apron, safety gloves, and a sturdy cap.

3. He practiced striking 10 matches, one at a time, waited to put out each match, doused each with water from the water can, and dropped them onto the grill.

4. Once he had finished with the practice, he cleaned the area, collected the fire-drill items, and stored them in the carport.

The entire fire-drill practice lasted approximately 15 minutes. This included retrieving the training items and clothing from the storage area and returning the items once the practice was carried out as intended. The training practice always took place under Mom or Dad's supervision.

To avoid conflict with his homework and school-related work, Bugsy was called to fire-drill practice only during his leisure time. Once he completed the practice period, he was free to resume his leisure time. This tactic also helped enhance Bugsy's motivation to complete the training as intended.

Within eight days of fire-drill training, Bugsy told his parents he did not think he needed to do the training anymore because he now knew how to safely strike matches. His parents told him that it would be possible to have a safety fire drill anytime he wanted to review his training. No more playing with matches was reported by his parents in a two-year follow-up. Bugsy seemed to have lost interest in playing with fire.

CHAPTER SEVEN

FOLLOWING INSTRUCTIONS IS A LEARNED SKILL

THE SCHOOL EXPERIENCE

If a child does not listen to nor pay attention to his teacher he will have some trouble learning academic material in school. When a child does not comply with requests to stop misbehaving and instead actively resists efforts to educate him, a teacher will shift her instructional efforts to other children. Over time, such a child is likely to find himself listless and bored in the absence of social and academic stimulation.

It is not enough for a child to be told what he is expected to do. He learns through hands-on training what the specific behaviors are that a given structure demands. At the pre-school or kindergarten level, for example, a child might be expected to quit using crayons or coloring and go on to wash his hands and then join his group on the carpet for story reading. While a child might prefer to stay with a given activity longer than that allowed, he is likely to contain himself and follow the teacher's instruction rather than do what he prefers to do. (It is in this setting that one can appreciate a teacher's skill in working with large groups of children.) Later on, in higher grades, children will find it easier to observe other rules.

Teachers judge children's misbehavior in terms of the degree of difficulty they manifest as they go from one setting to another, such as when they go from the playground to the classroom, or from one class to another.

Kevin and Freddy were first graders who enjoyed playing together. Their teacher was also pleased with their progress in academics and in conduct in the classroom. The problem was that when they were in the hallway going from the classroom to another classroom or activity, they often did not follow the teacher's established routine or instructions. They needed constant reminders and the teacher's supervision.

Transitioning from one activity and setting to another is not easy for some children. Because Kevin and Freddy continued going against the teacher's rules of conduct, they were regarded as having behavioral problems. However, by focusing on the structure within which misbehavior occurred, it was possible to check if and how that structure triggered the children's "battle" of the hallway.

School personnel often assume that a child is already socialized and will know how to conduct himself in school. When he does not, he is likely to be sent to the principal, and if he persists in his misbehavior, and defiance of the teacher, he may be put in time-out, given in-school suspension, followed by school suspension, and even expulsion. The problem is that trying to put a stop to defiance and misbehavior is not the same thing as teaching a child to behave well. He may be discouraged to misbehave for a time but if he has not learned an alternative, appropriate behavior he is likely to repeat the action that got him into trouble. School is the place where failure to follow instructions signals behavioral issues.

Justin, six-years-old, was an attractive little boy whose first-grade teacher was most concerned about his persistent misconduct in class. There was no question about his being smart and capable of following instructions. It was the way he failed to mind the teacher that posed a potential discipline problem. In short, Justin declined to follow the teacher's instructions and instead offered to do so if the teacher agreed to make a deal with him. He phrased his offer along the lines of, "What if I do X instead of Y?" Initially, the teacher tried to soften her own demands in an attempt to minimize classroom disruption. As Justin continued to try to make "deals" before he would comply with her instructions, she became concerned when another child began to pick up some of Justin's style of negotiation. Justin did not like that the teacher insisted on no deal and became surly and slow in complying with the teacher's instructions.

Interviewing Justin's parents revealed that his pattern of dealing with demands at home paralleled that displayed in school. At home he was typically good at having his parents agree to his "deals." In this manner it was easier for his parents to keep a semblance of peace at home and prevent Justin from becoming upset when a "deal" was not forthcoming.

There is no getting around it: a child needs to learn to

interact effectively with the schoolteacher by paying attention, listening to directives, and complying with the standards of classroom behavior and deportment. It is also clear that sometimes the parents' style of child management at home is working at cross purposes with the teacher's own expectations of classroom behavior.

It is to the credit of teachers that they have developed various and ingenious ways to assure that children learn to follow instructions and show respect for the teachers and other children. Parents are well advised to support such efforts to enable a child to become fluent in complying with routine requests at school. Unless parents emphasize socially appropriate behavior and respect for others, the job of a teacher and a child's progress are made all the more difficult. As parents are legitimately concerned about a child's school progress, it behooves them to learn what they can do to help.

LINKING PRIVILEGES AND PERSONAL BENEFIT TO SCHOOL PERFORMANCE

Most parents expect that children will want to learn and do well in school. Also, most school teachers do their best to encourage and support students' interest in learning. So why is it that many children are doing poorly or are underachieving?

Admittedly, the usual reaction to such news is to blame first the teachers, and next the school administrators. Also, the solutions offered include the usual cry for more money for buildings and resources or for more teachers. By now, however, given the current economy, it is unlikely these voices will find a receptive audience.

Because the problems of students' academic performance is not a new issue, it may be helpful to view this problem in a different way. Indeed, what is happening is that under-achieving students are not being held responsible for aca-

---

 Tip #11 | **To develop and improve appropriate behavior, link personal benefits to academic performance as well as to appropriate social behavior.**

---

demic achievement. To be sure, parents expect and teachers encourage children to do well in school. But, what happens when a child does well? Also, what happens when a child does not do well? Put in terms of the analysis discussed in this book, what is the personal benefit to the child if s/he does well in school versus the personal cost if s/he does poorly?

As matters stand, it is almost as if these children were satisfied with mediocre school performance and see little value in spending much time in school learning. In effect, one might speculate that the current consequences for above-average school performance are often absent. In fact, poor academic performance may not lead to any discernable difference in a child's personal cost/benefits. Under these conditions, it is unlikely that an underachieving child will improve academically.

Still, it should be pointed out that these children are not lacking in motivation.

Quite the contrary, they spend four hours or more a day watching popular culture as portrayed on TV or using the communication "toys" at their disposal including Facebook, texting, and so on. Their motivation is high on such activities. Everyone knows that if given a choice most of these children would prefer to keep doing what they are already doing . . . only more so.

HOLDING A CHILD RESPONSIBLE FOR ACADEMIC PERFORMANCE IN SCHOOL

Because most of the things that interest a child are to be found at home, parents can encourage a child to try his best in school by linking appropriate school performance to access to the "goodies" (privileges and personal benefits) at home. During the week, it is important to give a child credit for taking care of his schoolwork. All that is needed is for parents to request weekly feedback from the teacher as to a child's school performance. If he is doing average or above-average work, he should continue to enjoy his current fun time and be allowed access to the menu of privileges.

Parents can increase their expectations by gradually raising the standards of academic performance in order to earn the privileges and benefits. This routine increases a child's motivation to listen to his teacher and focus on what he is expected to do in class. When his teacher lets you know he is doing poorly in school, do not to take away his fun time. Rather, it is more effective to simply limit his fun time at home to about 30 minutes per day for one week. In a few days he will find out that his fun time at home is reduced to give him more time to do his homework or to practice reading and math skills as directed by the classroom teacher.

THE HOME EXPERIENCE

A child learns a variety of skills at home through modeling and guidance from his parents, including the rudiments of appropriate social behavior.

While it is less obvious, your child is also learning how you, the parent, handle yourself when he is pushy and argumentative. How do you react to his emotional outbursts? Are you easily manipulated? Do you cave in if he goes into some dramatic show of anger and aggressive behavior? How do you react to his refusal and defiance to stop misbehaving and do what you have asked him to do?

UNWANTED SIDE-EFFECTS FROM NEGATIVE CHILD-PARENT RELATIONS

The actions of a difficult child influence the way family members act and feel. Their actions, in turn, will have a reciprocal influence on the child's behavior. A negative cycle of actions and reactions surrounding household chores may escalate sometimes into verbal abuse and even physical aggression.

A child's refusal or failure to comply with parental directions has another and more pervasive effect. Specifically, when parents excuse a child from acting respectfully, they unwittingly prevent a child from learning cooperative, respectful, and responsible behavior.

Love is not enough.

For families to develop trust and family cohesion and to survive as a unit, they have to love and care for one another.

But love is not enough. Family members can come together through activities that unite them. That is to say, family members need to show their love by acting in helpful and respectful ways toward one another, toward their dreams, their efforts for self-improvement, and their accomplishments.

Parents know that something is wrong when a child's behavior is inconsiderate, irresponsible, and uncaring. Parents may be slow in admitting to themselves that things are not working out with a child as they hoped they would. Some may take a rather Pollyanna-like attitude about what's going on with a child. They may even be in total denial about the problems brought about by a child's attitude. But most parents are not deluded. Their inaction occurs because they often are not sure about what to do.

Setting limits is a necessary but difficult thing to do.

Often, guilt and worry consume parents' time and energy and weaken their resolve to bring discipline into a child's routines. Setting limits and enforcing them, such as bedtime, computer time, or television time make many parents uncomfortable. Yet, a child without boundaries learns to act impulsively, without a thought, when he discovers that his parents are uncomfortable, or too busy to say no to his demands. In general, as parents feel guilty and anxious when they limit or restrict a child's wants, he learns to ignore parental efforts to guide him. Gradually then, a child learns to act out aggressively, verbally, or physically toward others and often gets away with it. His noticeable lack of respect for others and for personal property is mostly the result of limited or inadequate social training. Often, this is exacerbated when parents are divorced and the lines of authority or house rules at home are unclear, or worse, absent. At such times, a child is most likely to rush in to fill the power vacuum and to impose his will.

Practice following instructions.

Learning to follow instructions and how to behave appropriately involves attention, focus, timing, and motivation to practice the skill. To develop and strengthen attention skills, a child needs exposure to a structured situation with a real-life context where he can practice a variety of focus-related skills. Family interactions at home provide a real-life context as they often revolve around household chores such as meal preparation, washing dishes, doing the laundry, vacuuming carpets, and so on. Chores are an important aspect of family living. They demand attention and require time, organization, and someone responsible for their being done. A structured home environment makes that possible.

Home is the environment where a child can acquire school-related skills through parental coaching. A frequent basis of parent-child interactions involves parental requests to help to pick up his toys, help put on his clothes, sit with Mommy, and help in other simple ways. A child learns through daily exposure to parental prompts and modeling to do specific things. Later on, parents ask a child to help keep the home clean and neat. Gradually, parents ask a child to pick up his dirty clothes from the floor, put his lunch plate in the sink, take out the garbage, feed the family pet, and so on. Some children are not only unmotivated to help with such chores but are highly resistant to parental entreaties. They protest, get angry, and often get into an emotional tug of war with Mom. At best, some children do not follow instructions as intended. They make errors of omission or commission, or both. They put on a good show, but that's all you can say. At worst, they find every possible excuse to skip doing what they agreed they were going to do. As a child continues to misbehave and simple rewards and punishments do not work, his problematic behavior will challenge a parent's resolve.

Skills fluency requires practice: lots of it.

In many ways, a child is constantly learning: mastering a musical instrument, playing ball, doing math, or exhibiting social skills. All of these endeavors require a teacher and a student. Also, they all require that the student practice on a regular basis to become fluent in the skills. Kids know about practice. They have practiced their ABCs, reading, writing, and arithmetic not to mention how to hit a ball, or how to do a handstand. The point here is that without practice or use it is very difficult to develop a skill and to maintain it. Most kids know that from their own experience. However, unless practicing the skill is fun to the kid, he will need additional motivation to practice. Effective teachers and coaches are aware of this, so they provide built-in consequences to practice and give feedback on skill development by rewarding small approximations to the skill at issue, and correcting for errors by including pop-quizzes, demonstration of skills in front of other students, try-outs, and so on.

The irony here is that parents expect children to remember their homework, chores, or their good manners with little and sometimes no special instructions, practice, feedback, or positive consequences.

WHAT TO DO WHEN YOU HAVE TRIED EVERYTHING AND THINGS HAVE NOT GOTTEN ANY BETTER

Let's say that you have tried everything you know to do and things have not gotten any better. Doing more of the same, even with greater conviction and intensity, will not work either. Typically, child and parent get locked into an emotional seesaw and neither seems to be able to stop the ride. Even after they move away momentarily and even after the emotional scene seems to have ended, something will spark the emotional reaction and reactivate it once again. Simple requests, commands, extensive talks, including rewards and punishment, are for the most part ignored, and helpful suggestions lead to endless arguments. No wonder parents rely on repetition of instructions and endless reminders to teach a child to mind. Yet, these children are neither deaf nor dumb. These children understand instructions perfectly well. That is why you have assumed that your child knows how to do what you have asked. Still, he has failed to do so. What is going on here? What happens is that a child's intellectual awareness of what is to be done is not enough. A child needs experiential awareness as well. Specifically, what happened when your child did not follow instructions? Through experience, he found that Mom or Dad would repeat the instructions, get tired trying and would finally stop bothering him for a while. Clearly, he needs an alternative experience: one that gives him and his family a chance for a more harmonious relationship.

Parents have to realize that a child does not reason his way into behavior. He often goes by feel, not through a thought process. True, as your own experience tells you, the usual types of reward and punishment are not helpful here. Still, the issue is one of motivation. We need to explore other ways of motivating a child to choose to follow instructions. Before we do so, it is time that you, the parent, change your mind-set, and act differently. You have nothing to lose and everything to gain.

Following are some guidelines to keep from repeating explosive emotional interactions.

- Do not yell or scream to get a child to do your bidding. A child will yell back and this will quickly escalate into an out-of-control emotional episode.

- Take a deep breath, in through the nose and hold it; slowly count to 15, and exhale. Repeat three times.

- Interrupt the conflict-laden situation (Excuse me, did you see my purse, keys?)

- Focus on something other than continuing with the conflicting scene.

- Move away to busy yourself with some other activity (make a phone call, peel potatoes, clean up your closet).

These guidelines will help you to defuse and neutralize unneeded confusion or anger. You now are ready to move more easily into a training program that motivates a child to learn to follow instructions at home and, in time, also in school, namely Tutorial Training.

TUTORIAL TRAINING FOR TASK-CHALLENGED CHILDREN

Quit all the reminders, begging, cajoling, demanding, and arguing to get a child to follow instructions. If he sees and hears well and there's nothing wrong with his brain, it's time to abandon those methods. Instead, regard his lack of cooperation as simply the result of deficient training on how to do the job he's been asked to do. Therefore, you concentrate not on your past experience with him, but you go forward with the view that the new type of training he is going to receive will also motivate him to do well.

CHARACTERISTICS OF TUTORIAL TRAINING

Tutorial Training assumes that there is only one reason for failure to do a task; namely, the child does not know how to do it. Therefore, to help a child, tutorial training is offered daily and has the following characteristics:

- It takes place at home.

- It emphasizes hands-on learning.

- It is slow and detailed to avoid pressuring or hurrying a child.

- It is offered during a child's leisure time. (It is not offered when the child is doing homework.)

- It is offered in the spirit of a loving parent helping a child to grow competent and responsible.

- It is discontinued when the child has completed the selected task to satisfaction for three consecutive times. Tutorial Training is resumed if there is need for a refresher or review period.

You are the job trainer. Take your job seriously. The child has developed "bad" habits as a helper. That is why you are going to use a hands-on-training approach and teach him in a straightforward fashion. Pretend he has never done the job. That should help you be a more detail-oriented instructor.

Practice a new "reaction" when your child ignores your requests. It is helpful to first select one or two things that he typically leaves undone despite your usual instructions to take care of such matters, say putting the breakfast dishes in the dishwasher. Once you have selected the task, you wait until he is home from school and is enjoying himself, perhaps playing a game on the computer. Go to him and interrupt him.

Say something like, "Hi Honey, may I show you something? It'll take only a minute and then you can get back to your game, OK?" If he goes with you, show him the dishes in the sink, and say something like, "They are still here. Please, take care of them now, OK?" It will help you to monitor how you sound. You do not want to sound angry or like a drill sergeant; quite the contrary. You want to sound loving, concerned, and congenial.

The chances are that he'll have a lot of excuses not to move from the TV or computer. If that is the case you now do the following:

1. Say, "That's OK, I can tell this is not a good time for me to be with you. Don't worry about it. We will work on it later." (All this is said in a soft and gentle manner in lieu of loud and angry talk. Remember: you want to sound loving and understanding.)

2. Move away from the situation but do not do the task yourself! Instead involve yourself with other chores or activities to indicate that you are busy and have no time to continue the above interaction. A child will not even notice as he is likely to be busy with his own thoughts or activities.

3. Wait until the child is enjoying his leisure time, having fun, watching television, playing video games, or playing outdoors.

4. Once again, interrupt his leisure or fun time.

Politely, in a soft and concerned manner, say, "Excuse me Honey. I know it's taken a while, but finally I have set aside time to teach you how to set the table before dinner (or put your shoes in the closet, or make your bed, or fold the clothes, et cetera). It is important that I show you how to do it. You see, it's not fair to expect you to know what to do if I haven't showed you how. I have been so busy lately that I just haven't had the time. So it's my fault. But now I have the time, so I am going to show you just how to do it, and then you can go back to your TV program (computer, and so on). It won't take us long, Sweetie."

Timing is key to the success of this routine. Think of the last time you were watching your favorite TV show and someone called you on the phone. Did you not make all kinds of excuses to delay and avoid being interrupted?

> 5. Choose one task so that you can get comfortable with the routine.

Taking the example of setting the table, break the task down into two or three steps. That means that you might ask him to take care of the cutlery only so that he can return to his fun as soon as he has done it. Later, you might increase the task to include glasses, plates, and so on. Remember you do not want to overwhelm him with your requests. You want the request to be doable. You want him to experience that leaving the task undone is likely to result in more interruptions in order to practice it to satisfaction.

A child will do his best to put you off, insisting he is busy, that he will do it later, and he will promise and try to convince you that you are not being fair. From his point of view, you are interrupting him at a very bad time. There will be many pleas for you to wait until his fun activity is over. Resist such pleas. After all, you have already set aside a certain amount of your time just to help him learn how to do the chore. Tell him it won't take but a minute for you to show him what needs to be done. Adopt a "broken record" quality in your talking to him. Insist that this is the only time that you have to teach him properly, and that it will not take long before he can resume his fun activity.

6. Again, do *not* do the task yourself!

When you begin to feel the tug of guilt, remember that his time is no more valuable than yours. The trick is not to argue, get upset, or participate in the match of wits he is expecting. Stay focused. Add action to your words. Stand in front of the television (computer game, et cetera). Position yourself in a way that he cannot comfortably continue what he is doing while you are talking. Very carefully and calmly define the task—methodically and calmly emphasizing that it is your responsibility to show him how to do the task.

7. He may fuss and say that he already knows how to do it. Keep your cool.

Just say something like, "No, I don't think you know how to do it because if you did, you would have done it, of course." Sometimes you might say, "All I know is that it has not been done. It is still undone." The purpose of these remarks is to avoid arguing the point. You simply describe what you see. For example, the dishes are still in the sink, or his clothes are still on the floor.

8. Remind him that once you show him how to do the chore he'll be able to return to his fun and games. Be sure that the chore is doable so that he experiences that doing what you asked him to do is a shortcut to getting back to his fun and games.

If he keeps resisting, respond to his remarks in a soft and understanding tone of voice.

9. Adopt a thoughtful look, and say something like, "You know something? I think I know why you had some trouble doing what I asked you to do." That may arouse his curiosity. He may wonder what you are talking about.

Explain that you assumed he knew how to do the chore and all you had to do was ask him or remind him to do it. You now realize that it is not fair to expect him to know how to do the chore. After all you never taught him. You might want to apologize for the fact that you have been working hard and been busy with one thing and another and just plain did not have time. But that is in the past. Now, you are going to make up for what you did not do before. This time you are going to teach him and give him practice time until he gets the hang of it. From now on, you will be available to tutor him as needed.

In short, a major reason for the child's problem in following directions was that you had not taught him how to do a particular chore properly. Blame yourself for having been too busy to do right by him. This is a new experience for the child. He fully expects to be blamed and is ready to defend himself and make it miserable for you in the process. By letting him off the hook, he now is more accessible to you. This is key.

10. Sound like a broken record.

If he insists he knows how to do the chore, just say, "Honey, if you knew how, you would have done it." Don't give in to his arguments to the contrary. Remain understanding and loving. Make him realize that he is wasting his time arguing because you will continue to sound like a broken record until he complies.

He will finally relent, and say, "Ok, Ok, Ok!" and ask what you want.

11. You are the teacher. Play it straight.

As the child starts the task, say something like, "I want to show you where the dirty clothes hamper is. Do you see it? Good! Your dirty clothes and towels go into the hamper". (Pretend he is a foreign student with little English at his command.) "Now we have to sort the clothes into light and dark. This might seem easy but I find that if I get distracted, I mix things up. Let me know when you are finished, and then you go back to your game (TV, computer)."

The idea is to have him spend about five minutes completing at least part of an assigned task and then let him return to his fun.

12. Allow him about 15 minutes of enjoyment of his leisure time. Then, interrupt him again.

This time he either finishes the task he did not complete before, or you include an additional part to the original assignment. The idea is to teach a child in a way that communicates your intention to be thorough in your method. He, on the other hand, finds such a thorough approach rather boring and he might add stupid. Remember, he failed to do the assigned task. This can mean that he really is at a loss as to how to do it. If he knew it, he would have done it long ago.

You have to teach him how to do the task that has yet to be completed, regardless of how haphazardly or reluctantly he may perform the task. Let him know that it takes time and practice to do a good job but you will be available if he has any questions.

Takeaway #18

The more parents "filter" out everyday inconveniences for a child, the less prepared he is to deal with even low-level frustration.

13. This is not a one-time event, which may explain why so many parents often relent and decide it's less work to complete the chore themselves. Don't give in, because in doing so, you do your child a disservice.

Keep in mind that the purpose of this type of interaction is to acquaint your child with household chores and to give him the experience to weigh for himself the personal cost/benefit of continuing to be inattentive and uncooperative. You may have to repeat the process several times before it sticks. Handle the approach the same way each time, starting with allowing him to settle into an activity that he enjoys before interrupting him. He will begin to know what is coming when you tell him that you now have the time to teach him and that it needs to be done now. Make sure that he understands what needs to be done, and he can resume his fun after the task is completed. Yes, he will be annoyed, and you may hear a variety of clever excuses. He might even say that he does not want to do it. Don't fall for that ploy.

He wants an emotional reaction to engage and distract you from focusing on the task. Respond coolly by saying something like, "I don't know about that. All I know is that you did not do it. But don't worry about that. All that means to me is that I have not done a good job of teaching you, and this time I intend to take more time to teach you properly."

14. Keep your cool, and be calm. Do not give him a speech about his being uncooperative.

    After a while, he will ask if this training is going to go on every evening. You may respond with something like, "Oh, no, we don't have to do this every evening. We only do it when you don't know how. Once you get the hang of it, there's no need for me to teach you and for you to practice something you already know how to do, right?" You want the child to experience you as helpful and understanding. Do not sound upset, worried, let alone angry. After all, you are only trying to be helpful. If he does not know how to do what needs to be done you will teach him practically the same day. If he already knows, he will need only to show it by doing it.

15. Stay focused on short-term benefits.

Through this routine, you are giving your child experience with the personal cost/benefit attached to his behavior. This experience enables him to make an informed choice. As he is routinely interrupted during his playtime and given an additional opportunity to practice what needs to be done, he will begin to weigh the cost/benefit of resisting change.

He has the opportunity to review his choices. He can choose to do the task at hand and stop your interruptions for training and practice. He also can choose to ignore your requests in which case you continue with the training program.

Tutorial training will work only if you do the following:

1. Stay calm, cool, and focused. You are sending a message that you are in control of yourself. Therefore, you are in charge of the tutorial training program.

2. Select his leisure time as the only time period when the training takes place.

   The time for training and practice in developing a skill takes place only during a child's leisure time when he is engaged in his own preferred activities such as playing outdoors, playing computer games, texting to his friends, and so on; in other words, when he is enjoying himself.

3. The training must not conflict with homework or school-related activities.

4. You interrupt your child during his leisure period and alert him that you finally have a chance to go over the situation with which he has been having difficulties.

5. Anticipate success within less than 10 applications of this procedure.

You are an understanding and loving parent but he is

annoyed by any interruption to his fun time. You reassure him that he can return to his activity as soon as you are able to show him how the task at hand is done. He may be in a hurry for you to get through with the teaching, but you are not. Take the time to explain how you learned to do the task when you were growing up. Share with your child how your mom, granny, or dad reacted to your own efforts. He'll hate your "war stories" because they take time and he wants to get back to his favorite activity as soon as possible. He will also be more motivated to get things done to avoid further and future tutorial training.

Tony's Experience with Tutorial Training

Tony was a delightful twelve-year-old boy with an older brother and a younger sister. His parents worked long hours every day and by the time they came home they needed some help from their kids. Tony was bright and interested in a lot of things. He was also rather skillful in not doing what he was asked to do at home. He neither put away his dirty clothes in the hamper, nor did he keep any semblance of order in his room. In summary, he failed to help with regular chores. Although Tony was quick to agree that his help was needed, he just never got around to do the chores assigned to him. The problem was that he put it all off until later when he was finished with whatever it was he was doing. In time, this situation escalated into his parents nagging, shouting, screaming, and making mild threats to take things away. Because his parents saw little or no change in Tony's efforts to help with household chores, they agreed they were ready to try anything that had a chance to work.

Tutorial training was explained to the parents and they agreed to try it. The focus was on giving Tony a special experience when he "forgot" to help with chores. Specifically, his mom undertook the job of teaching him the very chores that he had been assigned but had failed to do. For a child, such a solution is not fun. On the contrary, while he is being taught the skills involved in doing the chores, he is effectively taken away from doing fun things. This learning experience takes more time, more work, is terribly boring, and generally more inconvenient than doing the chores in the first place. It took about a week for Tony to decide to do his chores without all the hassle associated with it.

Increasing Tony's personal cost, in inconvenience, work, and boredom, when he "forgot" to do his chores solved the problem. In effect, Tony learned to "remember" to do his chores first to avoid Mom's tutorial program.

Children become quite proficient at manipulating their parents to comply with what they want. A child may complain, moan, or scream in an attempt to get out of a certain task. Also, he will try to make Mom or Dad feel guilty about requiring him to be responsible. In order to keep peace, parents often find themselves compelled to do nearly everything for a child in hopes that he will outgrow his dependency. With love and affection it is possible to have a child choose to learn to do things for himself because it is easier and less inconvenient than having a set time to practice what he already knows how to do!

CHAPTER EIGHT

REAL LIFE TEACHES RESPONSIBILITY

In an earlier age, the success of an agrarian economy depended on the active cooperation of the family members to engage in the caring and feeding of farm animals as well as on tilling the soil, seeding, and toiling side by side with family members. The farmhouse was the setting where a child gradually learned to perform these activities. Doing so enabled a child to be acknowledged for his help that, in turn, gave him a feeling of becoming competent and useful. As he was entrusted with activities that assured the comfort and livelihood of the family, he gradually grew into a responsible kid.

The farm is no longer the "natural" setting for developing certain family and social values. The major changes brought about by the introduction of sophisticated farming equipment eliminated farming as a way of life. Along with it went the farmhouse as the setting for creating a sense of belonging and personal responsibility.

However, the home is still the focal point for family interaction, and, potentially at least, it continues to provide the setting to teach responsibility through work and socially related skills. After all, the mechanics of living today still require that a variety of household chores be done daily. This offers a family an opportunity to relate to one another through their cooperative efforts to complete the chores. Yet, it is not sufficient for a child to help with chores. It is just as important that he learn to do his assigned tasks in a cooperative, considerate, and responsible manner.

Still, a child does not learn responsibility by osmosis. Rather, he needs experiences that involve personal cost-benefit for him where irresponsible behavior results in a clear cost to him in terms of effort, time, and energy. He does not have to be coerced to be responsible; he has to learn the behaviors that exemplify cooperating with his family. Cooperation with, and consideration for, others are at a premium when parents are under stress due to family issues or difficult economic conditions. In such cases, every family member is called upon to do his share of the work and to assist in reducing the material or emotional cost imposed on the family.

Responsibility is a by-product of doing things, or behaving in ways that parents or significant others regard as responsible. We know a child is responsible when he does something that his family appreciates, such as bringing the mail in from the mailbox, feeding the dog, handing in his homework, and helping with household chores. The point here is that it is through what we observe in a child's behavior that we conclude whether or not he is responsible.

Similarly, we can tell a child is respectful if he speaks appropriately to parents and significant others, allows others to speak, to have their own privacy, and so on. We know we're making progress in teaching responsibility, or respect, when we see children actively behave in ways that are responsible and respectful.

Chores and socially related skills are linked together. Household chores offer the medium through which the incidental teaching of socially related skills can take place. What exactly are the social skills we are talking about? We are talking about behaviors traditionally defined as polite, thoughtful, considerate, respectful, responsible, cooperative, and the like—all traits that are encompassed in the word civility. Most parents are concerned that a child behave politely, and to that end they often give feedback to a child as to the appropriate vocabulary to express their wants, for example, "May I, please?" "Thank you!" and so on. Social skills cannot easily be taught as memory drills. At best, they are taught incidentally as part of a family's living practices at home. To the extent that parents tolerate angry, loud, boastful, and generally boorish demeanor to that extent will a child live up to low standards of socialization.

Self-control is a learned skill.

Is there a safe and private setting where a child can be taught self-control? Parents realize that a public place is not the best place to teach a child self-control. Indeed, parents already know that they tolerate a variety of inappropriate and plain boorish behaviors when those behaviors occur in a public place. They do not like it but they also do not wish to create a scene, embarrass a child, or themselves, and aggravate the situation even further.

We are back to where we started. It seems that a child's own home may be the most suitable setting to teach self-control. Indeed, home also provides the setting to practice most socially related skills, including self-control. Daily family interactions often serve to spot early signs of a child's potential problems with self-control. Such opportunities present themselves when a child fails to follow task-related instructions or when he loses his temper and acts disrespectful to his parents. For the most part, difficult children are deficient in a repertoire of pro-social skills that includes following instructions. This is a basic repertoire in the absence of which parents, teachers, and significant others are prevented from assisting in the social development of a child and building on it.

Specifically, parents need to expose a child to the different consequences that flow from behaving in a cooperative as well as in a problematic way. This tactic empowers parents to establish house rules for the benefit of everyone in the family. In addition, it lays the groundwork for a child to become sensitive to parental expectations, and to learn about others' feelings and needs. By providing timely feedback to a child, the incidental learning of socially related skills is enhanced. Parents can then provide corrective feedback to a child and practice appropriate ways of behaving.

Disruptive, annoying, or defiant behavior characterizes a difficult child. Parents will typically suggest, instruct, or demand that a child stop his inappropriate behavior and conduct himself in an appropriate manner. But a difficult child loses his cool and cannot stop himself, often because he does not know how or because he is not motivated to behave appropriately. Either way, so long as a child's personal benefits are greater than his losses for losing control, he will continue to misbehave as he has in the past.

CONSEQUENCES MATTER

As you may have realized by now, a major tool that makes it possible for parents to communicate their concerns to a child is available through the use of consequences for behavior. For example, when access to any of the various privileges such as TV and computer games is linked to helping with household chores, a child is more likely to help. Meaningful consequences help a child get organized and replace his inappropriate behavior with appropriate behavior. A child's positive behavior naturally eases the strain and stress often experienced by hardworking parents and families in conflict. Eventually, a child learns to act in ways that are helpful, considerate, and respectful. The goal is to give a child experience with ways to gain control over his emotions. In this manner, a child gradually comes to internalize the positive feelings that go with meeting the standards of appropriate behavior.

Replace negative behavior with positive behavior.

To shift a child's behavior from negative to positive, parents need to develop, or amplify, appropriate social repertoires that will enable a child to experience positive regard and attention from his social environment. At the same time, it is vital that a child experience more inconvenience or physical effort (demand or cost), than gains for behaving negatively.

This tactic increases the odds that a child will be motivated to behave appropriately.

Parents often need additional options when dealing with frequently offensive, irresponsible, and impulsive actions. At such times, a strategy employed by parents and teachers to prevent further misbehavior is time-out, a routine that is often misused.

Time-Out from Preferred Activities: The Case of Sibling Rivalry as an Indoor Sport

A mother complained that her two daughters, ages six- and nine-years-old, were always fighting and arguing with each other. Both were smart and fun to be with except when they were together. Typically, Mom was called to settle the "argument du jour" but no matter what she did she could not bring ongoing peace and understanding between them. Often, they kept on arguing, pinching, pushing, and pulling even after they had agreed not to fight again!

The following routine involves a variation on time-out. The focus here is on, a) stopping the inappropriate behavior, b) redirecting it to a competing activity, and c) providing a specified time for peace and quiet for a child to regain self-control.

Take the following steps to effectively implement a time-out:

> a. Interrupt the flow of inappropriate behavior by re-directing a child from the ongoing stimulating situation to a non-stimulating, boring one.

b. Have the "offending" child go to a separate, quiet area where there will be neither distractions nor entertainment such as games, computers, and "goodies" in general. Some parents already use something similar, such as a "pouting chair," where a young child is sent when s/he misbehaves.

c. Regard this time period as a respite, a time for reflection, and peace and quiet. Allow the child to be by herself for a short period of time (depending on age, 5-20 minutes).

d. Skip the exhortations and speeches and resume your activities elsewhere.

Mother was advised to change her approach so that as soon as one of them complained to her, ("She hit, me!" "No, I did not! She hit me first!" "Tell her to quit!") Mom would agree that, clearly, they were not having a good time together. Obviously, they were tired of playing with one another and the best remedy for that was to take a five-minute break from each other. So Mom assigned each a rest area in the house where they would be alone and not be disrupted or bothered during their reflection period. For that reason, radio, CDs, computer games, and TV, were not allowed.

Within a short period of time, Mom reported notable improvement. Specifically, the girls rarely came to complain to her about each other. Even when they quarreled they managed to deal better with one another. What happened here is that a time-out period was imposed on both children. Specifically, what the time-out tactic did was three-fold.

1. It interrupted the flow of the fun activity and re-directed each child from the ongoing stimulating, "fun" situation to a boring, no stimulation, no "fun" one.

2. It prevented each child from making further contact with one another.

3. It provided each child with an opportunity to be away from the conflicting situation and to evaluate what to do next.

This routine put an end to the "fun" part of arguing with each other, and, prevented their shifting to an alternative fun activity of their preference.

Marc, a seven-year-old, lost his temper and threw an awful fit whenever his parents chose a nearby place to eat. Marc wanted to go to an eatery which was some distance away from their home. His parents had finally reached the end of their patience. Marc's Mom decided to use the time-out routine discussed here. Accordingly, next time he got upset with their choice of a place to eat, Mom told Marc that clearly he was upset and not feeling like going out. Perhaps, they could stay at home for another five minutes to see if he could get over being upset and in the right frame of mind to go out to eat. Meantime both parents went into the garden and enjoyed some quiet time together. After a few times of employing this routine, Marc stopped his fits and became more agreeable to his parents' choice of eating places.

HOW TIME-OUT WORKS

Technically, time-out is a behavioral technique that consists of removing a child from a stimulating to a non-stimulating situation for a short time (5-20 minutes) when he engages in inappropriate behavior. In effect, this procedure interrupts the ongoing inappropriate behavior for a set period of time at the end of which the child is free to return to his stimulating activities .

Stevie, a four-year-old boy, was sent to his room when he engaged in aggressive behavior toward his two-year-old brother. Each time this happened the child promised that he wouldn't do it again. Within less than 10 minutes, however, he took a toy away from his brother or pushed him as he went by. Philosophically, mother was against time-out. Therefore, the therapist suggested they stop using Stevie's room and use the hall as a place where Stevie could settle down when he got into trouble with his brother. Since the hall was bare, (no toys, games, or TV), it was a suitable place for Stevie to decompress and rest. At the end of five minutes he was free to resume his activities. Now, when Stevie promises he won't tease his brother again, his word is good for at least half a day!

WHEN TIME-OUT FAILS

Generally, in sports, time-out is a special period during which the player is afforded time to rest, away from the all-consuming physical exertion and stimulation, free to gain perspective of the game so as to re-enter the game revitalized. Unfortunately, this is not the way parents use time-out with their children. They typically use the bathroom where a child has a fleet of ships in the bathtub, or his room where he has his Nintendo, CD player, and other stimulating and rewarding activities.

That was the case with Ricky, a six-year-old boy whose parents were most disappointed because time-out did not work with him. In fact, he seemed to like it! Upon inquiry, they described Ricky's room as the time-out room where he had a variety of toys and games. This, of course, violates the very definition of time-out that rules out any contact with rewards and fun activities that offer a high level of stimulation.

MISUSING TIME-OUT AT HOME AND AT SCHOOL

Time-out is a well-known but poorly understood technique to discourage problematic behavior. Parents use it and so do teachers. Most of the time, however, parents and teachers complain that they have used it and it just does not work. Unfortunately, the conditions under which time-out is often used are not the ones that make this technique a viable one to discourage unwanted behavior.

MISAPPLICATION OF TIME-OUT AT HOME

A mother complained about her son's willfulness. It seemed to her that her eight-year-old son, Louis, was constantly argumentative and pushy. A counselor had recommended that she use time-out as an opportunity for positive interaction instead of just focusing on the unacceptable behavior. She did so and talked things over with him and let him know that she loved him. After using this time-out for about a month, she noticed that her son seemed to be more unruly than before.

What happened? The recommendation given to Mom was a mixed bag. It is important to let a child know he is loved and cared for. It is also important to give him opportunities to talk about what's going on with him and to listen to his experiences and dreams. However, using time-out to accomplish these very important goals defeats the purpose of the procedure that is to suspend stimulating interactions for a set period of time. This version of time-out selected unacceptable behavior as the one occasion that led to positive interaction with Mom. Not surprisingly, Louis continued, even escalated, his unacceptable behavior.

Most of the failures reported by parents when using the time-out procedure involve the shift from a stimulating (reinforcing) situation to another stimulating (reinforcing) situation. Time-out will work only when the child goes from a stimulating, interesting, fun situation to a non-stimulating, non-reinforcing, boring situation.

MISAPPLICATION OF TIME-OUT IN SCHOOL

Andrew, a twelve-year-old boy of normal intelligence, was a student at a private school for youngsters with emotional and behavioral problems. He had been expelled from public school the year before because of his highly confrontational and disruptive behavior. After three months of working with Andrew, staff in the private school was most concerned with his lack of insight into his problem. His teacher reported that he constantly annoyed her with his argumentative style whenever she tried to correct him. When advised that he should control himself, he became "almost like a lawyer" and challenged the teacher to show why he should do what she asked him to do. Finally, the teacher consulted the school counselor.

The counselor's advice consisted of two parts: Part 1 required that the teacher avoid giving Andrew attention when he behaved badly in class. Part 2 required that the teacher wait until it became clear that Andrew had lost control and could no longer be ignored. At such time, the teacher's aide was to take Andrew to a time-out room away from his classmates. There, the teacher's aide would talk to him, try to reason with him, and make him aware of the trouble he was causing others and himself. Despite these efforts, Andrew continued with his defiance and general misbehavior in school.

What happened? We should point out that part 1 of the above routine entails removal of attention-stimulating events. So far, so good. Part 2, however, presents a problem. While the intent was for the teacher to use a time-out, functionally, this is not what happened here. The teacher waited until Andrew's classroom misbehavior could no longer be ignored at which time the teacher's aide took Andrew out of the classroom and talked to him in private. The child was taken from one stimulating environment to another stimulating environment. That is not time-out. This routine unwittingly selected for attention, not just misbehavior but, rather a high rate of misbehavior. The well-meaning efforts by the teacher and her aide had the net effect of maintaining and once again, even escalating, Andrew's misbehavior. In short, when a child is in time-out, you want to avoid confusion.

1. During this period, stay busy and away from the time-out area. This is a period when a child has the opportunity to be in a quiet area by himself where he can do some thinking about his own behavior.

2. This is not a time to get emotional and discuss or rehash the past, let alone attempt to establish who is at fault.

3. Remain calm and wait until he gets to feeling better, more organized, and more self-controlled.

4. Return when the time is up and he is in a better place emotionally.

5. Avoid exacting apologies and promises to do better in the future. This can only provoke protestations about some perceived unfairness.

6. Once he is calm, go to his time-out area and ask if he is feeling better. If so, invite him to go and entertain himself while you busy yourself with your own activities (or in Andrew's case, return to classroom activities). Allow him to remain in time-out if he is still upset, since clearly he needs a little more rest time for himself.

Fundamentally, time-out is a technique that involves a dynamic cost-benefit balance. Inappropriate behavior does not go away by itself. A child must then have a good experience with appropriate ways of behaving.

PERSONAL COST (COLD PRICKLIES) AND BENEFITS (WARM FUZZIES) FOR YOUNG CHILDREN

In general, socially appropriate behaviors must be developed and strengthened to replace problematic ones. Parents often need a ready-made package of routines to encourage appropriate behavior, and discourage inappropriate behavior. Basically, growth experiences as well as self-corrective experiences are the stuff of life, particularly for a developing child. Following is a child-oriented version of the consequences a child experiences on a daily basis.

The "dynamic duo" involves the "warm fuzzies" (benefits) and the "cold pricklies" (cost) as consequences provided by parents. Each type of consequence influences a distinctive pattern of behavior.

"Warm fuzzies" (personal benefits) promote appropriate behavior and invite a child to make repeated contact with such situations. This results in an increase of appropriate behavior. For example, when Tex stored his bike as expected, Dad's positive reaction let him know he was really becoming a responsible kid. Similarly, when Carly showed Dad that she had done what she said she was going to do, Dad and Mom hugged her and told her they were very proud of her.

On the other hand, "cold pricklies" (personal costs) promote avoidance and invite a child to avoid or break contact with such situations. This results in a decrease of inappropriate behavior.

Mother talks to Brittany, an eleven-year-old girl

"We agreed that when you cleaned up your room I would give you a ride to the mall. Since you have not done it, I am not going out any time soon. Instead, I will be busy doing the laundry." As Brittany insists that she'll clean her room right away, Mom tells her that it's too late for that. Now she has to wait until the laundry is done which will take some time. However, Mom tells her if she wants to shorten the waiting time, she can help do the laundry.

Here, Brittany is given a second chance to go to the mall. However, now she has to straighten her room and help do the laundry. Next time, she is likely to avoid additional cost/effort (the "cold pricklies" experience) by shifting quickly to appropriate behavior.

In effect, self-corrective experiences offer children a choice as to the cost-benefits that are directly related to their own actions. This two-in-one strategy for behavior change decreases problematic behaviors while fostering and strengthening the emergence of socially appropriate behaviors that will replace the inappropriate ones. This tactic fosters self-control as a skill that allows a child to curb her inappropriate behavior (and the resulting inconvenience and discomfort it causes) because she now has acquired positive behaviors with which to replace it.

GUIDELINES TO ENHANCE A CHILD'S MOTIVATION: TRAINING REPLACEMENT BEHAVIORS

Children are unique. Some are temperamentally gregarious, others are shy, still others are fearful. Some children are highly competitive and get furious and lash out when they lose. Others are laid back and are not that interested in what their peers are doing. Some seem to enjoy the challenge and excitement found in doing things they are not supposed to do. Still, a child who behaves in problematic ways is also likely to behave in appropriate ways as well. Therefore, rather than dealing solely with the problematic behavior, the strategy proposed here consists of strengthening and amplifying a child's repertoire of appropriate behavior so as to replace inappropriate ones.

Allow natural consequences to be a child's best teacher.

In many respects, folk wisdom points to just this natural discovery: that one's actions have consequences that make it more likely for one to want to repeat some experiences and to want to avoid others. This point is conveyed through proverbs such as, "We live and learn," "Experience tests the truth," "Once bitten, twice shy," and the like. The functional property to be found in experience is that consequences teach. When a child is shielded from learning lessons taught by experience, he is left unprepared to deal with them the next time. Needless to say, meeting a child's safety and security needs comes first. However, we are not talking about situations involving such needs. Rather we are talking about daily events that test the patience and resolve

176

of parents and teachers.

The mother of Phil, a twelve-year-old boy, was informed by his teacher that he performed below his potential. It seemed that he did not return his homework on time or that his work was incomplete. Therefore, she had asked Phil to do a special library report. At home, Phil spent a good deal of his time watching TV or playing with his computer. When asked if he had any homework, he answered by saying that he had none or that he had done it already. When confronted with the teacher's concerns, he complained that the teacher just did not like him. He had done the work, so what was the big deal about turning his work in late? In the past, Phil's parents sided with him, since he was otherwise a well-behaved child. In the absence of natural consequences at home for failing to meet the teacher's expectations, Phil continued performing below the teacher's expectations. This parental inaction shielded him from getting in touch with natural consequences for doing poorly in school. These might include a daily restriction on the time spent playing games on his computer, missing his favorite TV program, or going to bed an hour earlier than the customary bedtime.

***

Eddy, an eleven-year-old girl, complained and berated her mother and pushed her plate aside when she did not like what Mom served for supper while yelling, "I can't eat this! I hate it. I want something else!" Eddy's mother tried in vain to persuade her to eat, but she just refused to even taste the food. Finally, to avoid making a scene at the dinner table, Mom placated her child and fixed something special for her.

This action reinforced Eddy's unpleasant mode of interacting with Mom. Furthermore, Mom shielded her from discovering some of the natural consequences that derive from refusing food. These might include getting hungry and learning to wait for the next meal, or having to fix a peanut-butter-and-jelly sandwich herself.

TAKING THINGS AND PRIVILEGES AWAY

Grounding:

Generally speaking, when a child continues to misbehave and act defiantly, parents can no longer tolerate his disrespectful behavior and are apt to ground him. Here, a child is no longer trusted to make the right choices of conduct and is given an extended time period to be away from his accustomed activities. This approach is in contrast to the one described previously that focuses on giving a child frequent opportunities to shift from negative to positive behavior.

While grounded, a child has neither access to TV, computer games, movies, nor friends to visit. In short, he is not allowed to leave the house except to go to school. Here is a partial list of activities, objects, and privileges that parents often take away:

1. Playing outside

2. Having a friend over

3. Entertainment in general (TV, sport events, musical events, and so on)

4. Access to electronic media (iPod, computer games, cell phone, and the like)

5. Selection of favorite clothing to wear to school (Nike shoes, boots, favorite T-shirt, sweatshirt, and the like)

6. Special services (optional trips to mall, selection of fast food places, favorite homemade meal on request)

Parents often feel that grounding gets their child's full attention. This is probably true. However, from the point of effectiveness, this approach is debatable. In fact, grounding may be counterproductive. For one thing, a child can adapt to the prolonged absence of a given item and no longer be motivated to do his best to get it. On the other hand, a child may try hard to show that he now comes home from school and does his homework, or cooperates with his parents, or does his share of chores around the house. However, if he has been grounded for three weeks, any quick positive changes on his part within the first week will not release him from his punishment until the three weeks are up. Once he finds out that his parents will stick to the three weeks of grounding, he is likely to give up trying and instead wait until the calendar gets closer to the three-week time limit before he makes efforts to show a positive change of behavior.

ALTERNATIVE WAYS TO DISCOURAGE INAPPROPRIATE BEHAVIOR

- One way to discourage inappropriate behavior is to arrange for the grounding to be of short duration such as a few days. This allows a child to choose to terminate the grounding as soon as he quits his inappropriate behavior and behaves appropriately.

- Another way to discourage inappropriate behavior is to curtail access to the menu of things and privileges a child is interested and actively involved in. For example, limit access to playing outside, or access to entertainment to 30 minutes per day for a couple of days. This provides a child with some contact with the personal benefits to be derived from behaving appropriately.

OVERPROTECTION AND THE RISE OF FRUSTRATION

A major issue for parents is having to deal with the pressure put on them by a child who has to have this or that at the mall, or has to be taken here or there, and now; not later, but right now! Such a child will not wait. He expects and demands to be given his due. He is used to instant gratification. Overindulgence has been the style his parents practiced as a way to develop a close relationship with their child. He may not have been born demanding, but by sparing him any inconvenience or frustration, he has acquired a demanding style of social behavior.

When parents overlook a mocking, defiant, and even aggressive attitude, they are training a child to expect that his wishes will be granted despite the offensive tactics he employs to convey his wants. When things do not work as a child demands he is likely to raise havoc. If things are still not working out for him, he is likely to quickly give up in utter defeat. Admittedly, he is ill-prepared to cope with frustration!

Parents are loving and protective of their children, and often shield them from having direct contact with the consequences of their actions. Typically, parents function as filters to the natural consequences of a child's behavior, buffering the child from inconvenient or unpleasant experiences. Even when a child calls Mom "stupid," "retard," or "bitch" Mom overlooks it or, at best, asks a child to stop his verbal attacks, to little or no effect. Such an approach tends to give a child "permission" to repeat this pattern of behavior with greater frequency and intensity. Over time, behavior that once was tolerated becomes more difficult for a parent to overlook or excuse. Furthermore, a child's contentious style of interacting with parents is likely to spill over in his interaction with other authority figures and settings, such as teachers and other school authorities.

Frustration management is a learned skill.

Multiple events can stress a child into acting irritated, annoyed, angry, and just plain frustrated. We are talking about events that a child will encounter in the course of a day, such as getting up early in the morning, missing the school bus, parents turning off the TV, eating at home instead of a favorite fast food place, doing homework on a timely basis, going to bed at night, and so on. It is part of the "mechanics" of living in the world that we gradually become adapted to daily inconveniences. It is unrealistic and also counterproductive to shield a child from ordinary, real-world inconveniences that produce feelings of frustration. We are not talking about overwhelming events such as a plane crash or a Katrina experience. It is largely parents who can teach a child to cope with the daily inconveniences and sources of low-level frustration and thereby help him develop his own sense of self-management.

Today's child seeks stimulation but avoids anything that might be frustrating.

Today's child has already discovered that the electronic entertainment and communication industries provide the quickest and most ubiquitous source of stimulation. The interactive features plus their speed and variety in content make them most interesting and stimulating for a child. Today's child is more of a thrill-and- stimulation seeker than children in the past, because today's electronic industry offers a child the quickest escape from frustration, boredom, and from listening to parents. Computer games and electronic devices with access to iPod, YouTube, MySpace, Facebook, texting, and so on enable a child to determine the kind and degree of environmental stimulation he wants. He now has the power to reduce or eliminate frustration and boredom altogether.

TEACHING FRUSTRATION MANAGEMENT

To teach a child the rudiments of frustration management, parents need to first review their own behavior. If they tend to overprotect a child, they are, in fact, preventing him from experiencing mild disappointments, and even low-level frustration. In the absence of experiences involving inconveniences and mild frustration, a child is altogether unprepared to deal and cope with minor irritations even those produced by his own actions.

Teach a child to do things for himself.

1. Rather than doing everything for a child, parents can help a child learn to do things for himself. As it happens, most children are structured around daily events. These involve waking up in the morning, dressing, washing, and getting ready to catch the school bus. They also include coming back from school, doing homework, having dinner, taking a bath, getting ready to go to bed, and going to bed. These real-life experiences are examples of age-appropriate activities and involve a good deal of instructions to learn to do for himself.

2. A child is often annoyed when Mom asks him to wait while she makes a phone call. Also, he may get upset, nag, complain, or start a fight when Mom asks him to help with chores. As she tries to teach him to do better she may frustrate him even more and unwittingly make things worse. Therefore, the teaching strategy is to first develop

the new self-management skills at home and then to transfer those skills to settings outside the home such as the school, mall, restaurants, and so on.

3. In the process of teaching a child something new, he will gradually be exposed to "baby" doses of frustration. As he learns to deal with mild frustration first at home and subsequently outside the home, these "mini" frustrating experiences serve to "innoculate" him against ordinary feelings of frustration he will encounter outside his home. In short, previously frustrating situations will no longer provoke the feelings they once did because he now knows how to cope with many such situations.

The Little Engine that Could Not: Benjamin, a six-year-old

Benjamin, a charming six-year-old, got easily frustrated and gave up when things got somewhat difficult. If he did not

---

 Tip #12 | **To teach a child how to cope with frustration, arrange matters for the child to make graduated contact with the natural consequences of his own actions.**

---

succeed immediately, he cried and complained until one of his parents righted the situation for him. "He just needs a lot of hand-holding, I guess," his mother said, adding, "He's been like that for some time."

One way of interpreting Benjamin's experience is that he

learned to act-emote-think helpless and to rely on his parents to get him through frustrating situations. His parents were coached to follow a special routine that exposed him to the typical frustrations inherent in the daily activities at home This allowed him gradually to learn to cope with them.

Most of the time, the context for learning coping skills is to be found at home in the daily opportunities to assist with household chores. Frustration management is an acquired skill and one that is not learned in one stroke or overnight. It takes practice for a child to learn to gradually tolerate frustration and to overcome his initial emotional reaction. Also, as most things at home are done daily through child-parent interactions, it falls on parents to be the natural teachers of the special skill of frustration management.

It should be noted that frustration management is a form of self-control or self-management. It is his outburst or angry behavior that people notice and find objectionable. The focus on changing first the child's outward behavior allows him to notice what it is that people are reacting to. The next change is not easily apparent to others but it may be to a child. Internal change is possible in terms of thoughts and feelings that allow a child to feel the difference in people's reaction to his more restrained manner of interacting.

SOME THOUGHTS THAT HELP ALMOST LIKE MANTRAS!

1. Quit thinking that you give your child self-esteem. FOCUS instead on encouraging skilled

and competent behavior as the road to gaining self-esteem.

2. Quit talking and reasoning to teach your child respect and responsibility. FOCUS instead on direct, hands-on, experiential avenues that promote respectful and responsible behaviors.

3. Quit shielding your child from the consequences of his inappropriate behavior. FOCUS instead on his having direct contact with the natural discomfort and annoyance produced by his own misbehavior.

4. Quit rewarding a child for angry, nagging, irresponsible behavior. FOCUS instead on the self-corrective experience of confronting his own frustration and anger.

CHAPTER NINE

WHEN CONSEQUENCES DO NOT
SEEM TO WORK

A major basis for the failure of consequences to work as intended involves three components: the availability of personal benefits, the level of behavior (skill) to access benefits, and the linkage between behavior and its outcome.

THE AVAILABILITY OF PERSONAL BENEFITS

When the consequences are parent- rather than child-selected, their effectiveness is seriously compromised. For example, an adolescent boy was offered a chance to attend a concert of classical music if he finished his homework by 9:00 p.m. for one week. Although he was able to do his homework one out of five days, his parents were disappointed that their son failed to meet their expectations. However, since the only music he liked was country music, it was not surprising he showed little interest in doing his homework for the chance to go to a classical concert.

THE LEVEL OF BEHAVIOR OR SKILL
TO ACCESS PERSONAL BENEFITS

At other times, the problem has to do not with the consequence itself but rather with the degree of effort or skill involved in meeting the required behavior. For example, it is not helpful to promise to go to the park for reading a book if a child's reading is not yet fluent. However by taking "baby-steps," and gradually increasing reading from three to five to eight pages for the child to be taken to the park would encourage a child to read. In time, reading would allow a child to enjoy the content of the book: the story.

THE LINKAGE BETWEEN BEHAVIOR
AND ITS OUTCOME

When the outcome of the behavior is selected by the child and the level of effort and skill for the task is age appropriate, the only other issue concerns the linkage between the behavior and the outcome. Although the emphasis is on immediacy between the behavior and the outcome, in actual practice this is typically achieved during early training of the skill or behavior. For example, in pre-school or kindergarten, and even in first grade a child may get immediate feedback such as a happy face to encourage appropriate behavior. Soon thereafter, however, a child will be told that meeting certain established social or academic requirements will result in a satisfactory or excellent mark.

The same approach will likely be followed when a child takes language skills or math where the grade may be a mark, a point, credit, or token. The token or point system has been well established and allows for a great deal of flexibility in exchanging these points for items from a menu already known to a child. A word of caution regarding symbolic feedback such as happy faces, points, chips, tokens and the like: unless these are exchanged for items that are of interest to a child, their effectiveness is temporary and often limited to their being a novelty.

WHAT TO DO WHEN PROBLEMATIC BEHAVIOR PERSISTS

Three possible reasons account for difficulties and failure in changing a child's behavior. As discussed above, problematic behavior may persist due to a skill deficit, a motivational deficit, or a disconnect between behavior and its outcome.

SKILL DEFICIT

To determine the type of deficit involved, it is useful to ask two basic questions:

1. Does a child know how to do what he is being asked to do? Yes or No

2. Has he ever done what he has been asked to do? Yes or No

If the answer to both questions is, "no" or, "I'm not sure," the likelihood is that reinforcement alone will fail to change a child's behavior, and reinforcement is needed to train the required skill.

What to do: Train the required skill or replacement behavior.

The solution lies in either skill training, or in shaping the appropriate replacement behavior. If a child does not have the skill at issue he will have a chance to learn it. This is the case even when a child insists he knows what to do or how to behave. The issue is not what he knows but that he shows through his action what he knows. The cases of Silent Sammy (page 12) and Tony (page 159) illustrate this approach.

MOTIVATIONAL DEFICIT

Again, to determine the type of deficit involved, ask the two basic questions:

1. Does a child know how to do what he is being asked to do? Yes or No

2. Has he ever done what he has been asked to do? Yes or No

If the answer to both questions is, "yes," or "I'm not sure" the likelihood is that the problem is one of lack of motivation. That is to say, a child sees no personal benefit in complying with Mom's instructions. In fact, it is possible that compliance with Mom's instructions could take place only at a personal cost to him. Therefore, a child will behave in a variety of ways so as to avoid compliance with Mom's instructions. For example, a child knows what to do and how to behave but, "just don't wanna" because he sees no benefit or only a cost for behaving appropriately. In a sense, a child says to himself, "Why should I do it? It doesn't make any sense. I'm not going to do it!"

What to do: Increase the benefits for behaving appropriately and reduce the inconvenience/cost attached to it.

A DISCONNECT BETWEEN BEHAVIOR AND ITS OUTCOME

Ask two basic questions:

1. Is there a linkage between a child's behavior and its outcome? Yes or No

2. Does the outcome/consequence follow the selected behavior? Yes or No

If the answer to both questions is "yes," the likelihood is that the problem lies elsewhere.

What to do: Make sure that the menu of personal benefits comes from the child and not from the parents. Is that the case?

If the answer is "no," or "I'm not sure" the problem lies in the linkage between behavior and its outcome.

What to do: Arrange the situation so that the outcome follows the selected behavior.

A nine-year-old girl, Clara, had frequent quarrels with her parents over her slowness and general lack of cooperation in getting ready for school in the mornings. Often, her parents were under pressure to get to work on time and still had to spend time to coax and cajole Clara to get dressed and get going. Once her parents instituted a point system that rewarded her for being ready on time to catch the school bus, she no longer dilly-dallied or argued with her parents about being sleepy, tired, et cetera. She simply dressed herself and, as she merrily left to catch the school bus, reminded mother to credit the agreed-upon points to her account!

> **Takeaway #19**
>
> **A child tends to repeat behaviors that meet his needs for love, attention, physical contact, and emotional connection to parents.**

This dramatic change occurred within a week, following several months of ineffective arguing over the same issue. How is that possible? Clara already had the required skills: she knew how to dress and get ready for school.

In short, her parents needed to increase the sources of positive reinforcement/consequences to include not just attention but also personal benefits for behaving appropriately.

CHAPTER TEN

THE POWER OF PRAISE

Research data shows beyond doubt that behavior becomes more likely to reoccur when it leads to good outcomes. This particular effect has been found first with laboratory animals, as well as with a wide range of species. Starting in the 1950s the application of this principle was initially extended to difficult populations such as the severely mentally ill including the retarded, autistic, and schizophrenic patients as well as prison inmates. Because of their behavioral as well as cognitive and emotional limitations and deficits, there was little if any expectation of progress for some of these individuals. Surprisingly, the data again showed that behaviors that were followed by desirable events became much more frequent than those that were not. Further, the data showed that along with the behavioral improvement often came positive emotional changes as well. Since then, the application of this principle of positive reinforcement to a wide range of human activities and environments has been widespread including education and business. Further applications have been made in the medical area including issues involving babies, children, and adults. Still, there is a surprising misunderstanding about how reinforcement works. While the overwhelming amount of research data indicates that a desired result increases the behavior that it follows, somehow, in practice this principle has often been implemented incorrectly or has been distorted. Perhaps this is an appropriate place to clarify a series of misunderstandings that often confuse parents and even teachers.

Misunderstanding #1: The use of rewards relies on bribing a child with M&M's and other incentives to change behavior.

This is a frequent misunderstanding. For example, the parents of a three-year-old little girl who was not toilet trained praised and offered her a "treat bowl," containing an assortment of candies to choose from after she went to the toilet. Soon after she learned how to use the toilet, she forgot about the treat but continued to use the toilet successfully. That should not be surprising. After all, her newly acquired skill expanded her social world to include pre-school and public settings. It is these new social "connections" that are now the natural rewards for the new skill. Also, from time to time, she announced her being proud of now being a "big girl," and not a baby.

Surely, incentives have a place in motivating a child to try tasks that are of no interest, difficult, or boring but are developmentally or socially beneficial to a child. It must be kept in mind that the usefulness of consumables, such as M&M's, and other goodies, is largely transitional, and limited to achieve short-term goals.

Misunderstanding #2: Rewards are unnecessary and likely detrimental.

A mother complains, "Why should a child be rewarded for doing what he's supposed to do in the first place? That's not right!"

Some parents believe that it is unrealistic and morally reprehensible to put into practice a system that is built on rewarding good behavior. The belief is that a child knows what to do and how he should behave. Therefore, he does not need any special reward for doing so. He should just do it; that's all. Of course, the problem is that a child just does not do as instructed despite the fact that he knows what he is expected to do. As discussed previously, the issue may be one of simply not wanting to do as instructed in which case motivation has to be addressed. On the other hand, if there is reason to believe the child has not been taught or his skill is defective or faulty, it would be appropriate to assist him by designing a learning program that would help him to take "baby steps" in acquiring the selected skill. To achieve this goal, a child's motivation has to be addressed once again.

In short, positive or negative attention is ordinarily what is involved in working with a variety of problems presented by children. It could be said that such children have been unwittingly reinforced by parents' efforts to correct the unwanted or inappropriate behaviors. What is clear is that in a majority of such cases, these problems owe their maintenance to the parenting practices at home.

The question then is not about whether a parent should or

should not reward a child. Parents already do and do so daily and many times a day. The issue is that the concept of reward has been misunderstood to mean prizes, goodies, even money. For practical purposes, the concept of reward for children has to include the linkage between a child's behavior and the parental reaction to it. By so doing we empower parents to, first, examine their impact on a child's behavior, and second, to extend their effectiveness in promoting positive behaviors rather than counterproductive ones. Praise is most effective when it follows appropriate, organized, constructive, cooperative, responsible, and helpful behavior.

Misunderstanding #3: The real reward for a child is the feeling inside him.

Parents employ rewards to foster the right feelings (feeling loved, feeling happy) because they believe such feelings will also persuade and motivate a child to act right. Feelings are most important. For example, positive feelings are likely to be produced when a child does something that results in parental approval, hugs, and kisses. On the other hand, somewhat negative feelings are likely to be produced when a child does something that provokes parental indifference or critical remarks. In future situations, a child is likely to approach situations that resemble the positive experiences in a free and relaxed manner (with positive feeling). On the other hand, he may approach situations that resemble the negative experiences in a somewhat inhibited or cautious manner (with negative feeling). Here, the emphasis is on the consequences or outcomes that follow behavior, and feelings are a by-product of the behavior-consequence process.

What is the advantage of thinking of feelings in this way? The advantage is that it allows parents to know how to help develop positive feelings. Parents cannot order a child to have a positive feeling. What they can do is interact with a child to encourage positive feelings. They can do that by focusing on constructive, appropriate, helpful, organized behavior, and making positive comments as they see a child behave in such fashion. Over time, a child develops a positive feeling as a by-product of this behavior-consequence process. He is likely to repeat such behaviors because the consequences (the attention, love) for so doing please him.

Misunderstanding #4: The trouble with using rewards is that a child will quit doing the desired behavior once these rewards are withdrawn.

That is not so! In fact, research indicates the opposite. Continuous reinforcement must shift to intermittent reinforcement once behavior has been developed. In practical terms, long-term performance can only be sustained if the rewards are no longer given frequently but rather infrequently. By that time, the activity acquired through rewards may continue to occur because the motivation is now more complex involving personal cost/benefits that may now include internal as well as external ones.

Misunderstanding #5: If a child wants to learn, she will learn. There is no need for rewards.

Sometimes a child is willing to put a lot of effort and time into some chosen activity because she believes achieving her goal is worth the struggle. Other times, a child may not have enough exposure to, or interest in, acquiring a skill such as playing the piano so she may not even try. For her to be motivated it might be useful to reward and praise her for playing the piano. However, as she learns to play the piano, she is no longer dependent on "goodies" or parental praise to continue playing. That's because now the activity itself, playing musical pieces, is the natural reward for the child. She likes to hear herself playing. It "feels" good doing it even when her parents do not praise her for it. What keeps a child playing the piano may now include the feeling of competence, or of relaxation, and possibly the feeling that she is making new friends.

Misunderstanding #6: Rewards don't work with smart kids.

Rewards will not work with either smart or not-so-smart kids if those rewards are not kid-friendly. Often, the choice of rewards reflect the taste of the parents rather than the kids' own. For example, a child was offered a special treat for doing homework. Specifically, he was given a chance to go fishing because Dad liked fishing. The child, however, thought fishing was terribly boring and had a variety of excuses for not going fishing with Dad. Not surprisingly, going fishing did not improve his homework. This was not a reward for this child but a reward for Dad.

Misunderstanding #7: Rewards increase one-note, mechanical-like types of behaviors.

This is simply not true; quite the contrary, in fact. When parents give their child positive feedback and recognition for behaving in a polite manner at home, he is learning a polite "style" of behavior which includes variations on "polite behavior." In other words, he is not learning a single, polite response. Over time, he is learning a set of skills that make up a pattern of "polite" behavior that he is able to employ outside the home where he discovers that people react positively to such behavior.

Misunderstanding #8: Praising a child as often as possible builds self-confidence.

This notion seems to have resulted in over-parenting. In the belief that self-confidence is the engine of success, parents make their mission to build self-esteem in a child. They praise a child as often as possible. Praise is a kind of positive reinforcement, and of major importance to parents. The belief is that praise will lead a child to succeed academically and socially. Therefore, parents are often made anxious when their child is not doing as well academically as they think s/he should. They are apt to demand from the teacher some kind of report about her lessons or about her frequency of praising their child. All this drama is based on a fundamental flaw. Rather than increasing positive behavior, over-praising can decrease positive, constructive behavior. As a child hears the constant refrain, "good job," and variations on the theme of, "You can do anything you put your mind to," despite the fact that he is doing poorly in school, he comes to believe he is special and entitled to expect special treatment from peers or teachers. As time passes, he may even become confused and upset as he discovers that peers or teachers are not impressed with his harboring such expectations.

If parents praise a child in the absence of any linkage

between some specific behavior on his part, the praise will not result in a predictable increase in his doing homework or helping with household chores. In short, simply telling a child "Good job! or "You are great!" is not as effective as specifying what the "good job" or what the "great" refers to. For example, a parent might say, "I noticed you put the dishes in the sink and scraped and rinsed the food off of them. I like that. You really are helping me, Honey!" This describes a child's specific behavior and a mom's reaction to it (praise). The likely effect is that it will increase a child's behavior. But this process does not stop there. Because a mother and child have a reciprocal influence on one another's behavior, the child helping in the kitchen will also increase a mother's own behavior of praising him.

Praise is not the issue. For praise or rewards to be effective, parents and teachers must assure that it is the outcome of a specific behavior. That is to say, praise that follows a specific behavior will likely increase its frequency. For example, a parent might praise a child when he finishes his homework before supper rather than after supper. The likely outcome of such efforts will be an increase in doing homework before supper. This is in contrast to Mom praising a child without reference to any behavior. Although excessive praise is to be preferred to its total absence, it also can lead an overprotective parent to produce unintended results.

Misunderstanding #9: Happy faces, stars, and tokens are just for kindergarten.

A mother complains: "I've tried rewarding my child with happy faces (stars, points, tokens, bracelets, credits, and the like) and after a few days the novelty wears off and those items do not work anymore."

These complaints derive from a technical misunderstanding. Points, happy faces, and so on, are not the "real" thing. They are symbolic items that have a rather short shelf life. They do not last. Their effectiveness is at best limited to their being a novelty. Compare this situation to trying to tempt someone with Confederate money from the Civil War or with European money such as francs or lira that are no longer in circulation. Today, these currencies are a novelty, but nobody would exchange these currencies for real goods. All of these currencies live and die depending on whether they can be exchanged for the "real" backup items.

In the case of schools, the various symbolic items employed by teachers derive their effectiveness from the opportunity to exchange them for back-up items, such as free time, access to student choice of computer program, use of an iPhone, and so on. Similarly, at home, the power of symbolic items derives from a menu of possible back-up items and activities including play time, TV time, bike riding, playing in the park, and so on.

SUMMING UP

Parents may feel benign and loving in continuing their well-meaning efforts in parenting a difficult child. However, if the child persists in behaving poorly it is possible that the parenting style is no longer a potential solution. In fact, it may have become the problem.

After reading all about these problematic behaviors you

might wonder, Is there a common denominator to them? At first look there is not. But if we now focus on the social context within which a child's behavior emerges, we will find major core principles that influence the behavior of both parent and child. These are as follows:

1. The reciprocal influence of child-parent interactions

This influence is mutual and it operates through their action and reaction toward one another. In a real sense, parent and child "teach" one another how each will respond to the other. And just as important, they also "teach" what to think and feel about one another.

2. Consequences

Consequences are natural when they flow from the unique characteristics of the problematic behavior and the parents' typical efforts to manage it. In actual practice, these natural consequences are often socially defined. For example, in Western-oriented countries a nine-year-old sleeping with his parents is frowned upon and discouraged. In other cultures, the whole family, babies, growing children, and parents, may enjoy sleeping together.

Other consequences are those imposed by the physical environment. For example, a child may start a fire despite his belief that he is just playing with matches. The natural consequence, a physical one, is the likelihood of a fire when playing with matches. That is an issue of much concern to the parents.

Generally speaking, it is the socially defined consequences that are most often at issue in the development and maintenance of disruptive and counterproductive behaviors. The approach discussed here allows us to focus on the customary reaction to a child's misbehavior to better understand how it develops, persists, and how it can be altered.

3. Choices

Choices minimize a child's natural resistance to change. To discourage and control disruptive and counterproductive behaviors, parents are likely to block or impede further misbehavior through punishment or coercion. While such efforts are understandable, the results may be temporary and also provoke unnecessary conflict and anger. An effective technique to encourage change is to provide a child with some choice and the accompanying sense of control over the consequences attached to each choice.

4. Meaning

The meaning of a child's actions is of concern especially to parents and teachers. They want to understand why the child acts the way s/he does because they want to help. Typically, their focus is on the internal workings of a child's mind. This might seem to offer a shortcut to the task at hand. However, the flight into an examination of the mind makes it difficult to know when one has arrived at one's destination. For example, does the child misbehave because s/he is lazy, has low self-esteem, or is it because s/he is manipulative? Perhaps s/he misbehaves because s/he has a special condition such as Hyperactivity, Attention Deficit Disorder, Separation Anxiety, or School Phobia. Unfortunately, such labels do not readily lead to an analysis of the social context within which misbehavior emerges, persists. and from which it derives its meaning. Therefore, one must exercise caution in the use of such labels particularly with an impressionable child. S/he can come to believe in and identify with the label and gradually become even more resistant to change.

From a practical viewpoint, the whole process of delving into the mind is enormously time-consuming and not subject to timely verification. On the other hand, the strategic parenting approach discussed here provides a kind of road map for parents to gain access to the meaning of a child's misbehavior by tracing it to the personal cost-benefit consequences that trigger and flow from misbehavior.

A STRATEGY FOR PARENTING

Although change can also come from the inside out, the focus here is largely on change from the outside in. That is because a parent is largely limited to promoting behavioral and emotional change by modifying the parental practices that impact on the child's behavior.

To change a child's problematic behavior, it is necessary to identify where and when it takes place, and what the related consequences are that follow it. Typically, these consequences involve parental attention and through it a difficult child learns to exert some control over parental decisions. The focus is on altering the parental consequences to discourage inappropriate behavior and encourage a child's appropriate behavior.

Change requires a strategy in order for it to be effective.

A strategy is a concise plan of action to be achieved over a span of time. And the plan of action needs to be mapped out, rehearsed, and adhered to. A strategy is not an instant fix. It requires consistency and discipline. While this approach appears cut and dried, the fact is that parents are not always aware how, where, or, when a child "picked up" some undesirable behavior. Therefore, they are often at a loss to determine why a child persists in his misbehavior, and how to deal with it. At such times, it is particularly helpful to identify the "purpose" of a child's behavior by finding out what it is he gains or avoids for so behaving. Simply put, what does the problematic behavior do for him?

A popular and valuable strategy is to encourage a child to share his feelings and thoughts since in doing so he may give clues as to where, when, and with whom he has daily interactions that encourage or discourage appropriate behavior. Sometimes, this may help parents to trace a child's unusual emotional reaction to the unwholesome influence of a peer group.

Techniques to discourage misbehavior do not, by themselves, maintain appropriate behaviors. Problematic behavior is most likely to return in the absence of positive reinforcement for appropriate behaviors. It is important for parents to understand how they influence a child's behavior through their daily interactions. As it happens, a child will engage in "good" or "bad" behaviors more frequently depending on the personal cost/benefit outcomes for so behaving. To bring about change, parents must be mindful of their role as providers of consequences to a child's behavior.

The most effective strategy to change a child's behavior is to increase the odds of appropriate interactions and to reduce the likelihood of inappropriate ones. To achieve this goal, it is useful to employ a mix of positive and self-corrective consequences. The strategy proposed here remains consistent, both conceptually and procedurally, with an overall approach that acknowledges the powerful influence of the current social environment in understanding and changing behavior. It should be noted that this process of behavior change works even when a child or his parents are unaware of their role in it.

INTERACTIONS THAT PROMOTE POSITIVE BEHAVIOR AND SELF-ESTEEM

A child needs to see, hear, and feel positive expressions of love and support as they relate to his efforts to act in a loving, cooperative, and respectful manner.

There are three elements involved:

1. The timing of such expressions. He needs your reaction to his constructive efforts as soon as you become aware of them.

2. The touch as a way to "anchor" the positive verbal expressions to the specific behavior. He needs a pat on the back. When you do that, he is more likely to repeat the action that resulted in your positive comments because his body carries a memory trace of the event.

3. The talk can take the form of attention, acknowledgement, approval, acceptance, and affirmations. When should these positive consequences take place? Ideally, such positive attention should be given when the child is saying, doing, or acting in a manner that is cooperative, constructive, creative, helpful, organized, competent, useful, on-task, focused, affectionate, loving, respectful, or considerate.

In other words, the timing for positive attention/positive consequences is whenever you catch the child behaving in any of the above ways—when s/he gets up in the morning, before s/he goes to bed, when s/he returns from school, before and after meals, and so on. Where do you give the positive attention? The answer is wherever you catch the child behaving well be it at home, in the car, at the mall, at the supermarket, and so on.

SPECIFIC STEPS TO PROMOTE SELF-ESTEEM

Positive Reactions to Help a Child Develop and Strengthen Self-esteem.

A child needs to hear positive expressions of love and support including a pat on the back.

When?

When s/he is saying, doing, or acting in a manner that is, cooperative, constructive, creative, helpful, organized, competent, useful, on task, focused, affectionate, loving, respectful, or considerate (select the adjectives that best express your reaction).

Time?

Anytime you catch him/ her behaving in any of the aforementioned ways

When s/he gets up in the morning, and before s/he goes to bed, when s/he comes back from school, be fore and after meals, etc.

Where?

Wherever you catch him/her behaving in any of the above ways

At home, riding in a car, at the mall, supermarket, etc.

What to say?

Variations of any of the following as appropriate (fill in the blank)

- It makes me feel good when you _____.

- I'm so proud to see you_____.

- You really know how to _____.

- It's not always easy, but you completed the _____.

- I like it when you help with _____.

- It's so nice to hear you say_____.

- When you do your homework, chores, etc., as you did _____.

- You really show your stuff.

- I like it when you ask me in a soft and friendly way.

GUIDELINES FOR PARENTING: UNDERSTANDING A CHILD'S BEHAVIOR

Everything a child does involves an integration of feelings, thoughts, and actions–all largely learned first in interaction with parents.

The meaning of a child's behavior is socially nested at home, school, and with his peers.

A child tends to repeat behaviors that meet his needs for love, attention, physical contact, and emotional connection to parents.

A child seeks negative attention when he feels he is not getting enough attention through appropriate behavior.

Unwanted behavior persists when personal benefits outweigh personal discomfort, or effort.

When a child repeatedly fails to follow instructions and avoids tasks or situations s/he also gains control over a parent's behavior.

Overprotection encourages dependent, and/or irresponsible behaviors.

A child learns to rely on parents and significant others to rescue him from self-produced discomfort and annoyance.

The more parents "filter" out everyday inconveniences, the more a child relies on parental help.

Overprotecting a child tends to disconnect behaviors from their natural consequences.

Rescuing a child from repeated self-produced discomfort further encourages it.

PARENTAL PRACTICES THAT ENCOURAGE MISBEHAVIOR

Overlooking repeated misbehavior functions as tacit approval and further encourages it.

Placating a child when s/he misbehaves encourages more misbehavior.

A child will experience stress and act inconsistently when parents do not agree on setting limits and boundaries.

Appropriate and inappropriate behaviors are learned.

Parents do well to focus on appropriate behavior or otherwise they will be focusing on inappropriate behavior.

Misbehavior is learned, but can also be unlearned.

Helplessness is learned, but can also be unlearned.

Irresponsible behavior is learned, but can also be unlearned.

Parents get the good (or bad) behaviors they accept.

Parents are often given little credit for the difficult task of juggling all the demands made on them. At some point they simply are exhausted from work and by the time they come home they do not have the energy to do more than either accept what the kids are doing or spend their time correcting and disciplining them. Not surprisingly, faced with the choice, they prefer to avoid arguments and emotional confrontations. It is not that they are happy with this choice. Rather, they believe that by avoiding making a scene, things are likely to get better. This only postpones the day when parents discover that they no longer have control of the child. The child basically acts as his own boss. In fact s/he masquerades as an adult!

In recent years, the popular media has introduced parents to the benefits of using a positive approach to foster appropriate, adaptive behavior in children. Parents have also been cautioned against the potential psychological harm that may ensue when relying on punishment to stop a child's maladaptive behavior. These general notions are loosely derived from a structured, evidence-based, approach to child behavior and its management.

We have seen from case to case and example to example that the behavioral routines described here demonstrate a relative ease of implementation. Still, the transition from the familiar ways of interacting with a difficult child to adopting a more nuanced style of relating requires patience and practice. Active child management rather than passive acceptance of the status quo also requires commitment to change.

The specific set of guidelines discussed here provide the details of a systematic approach to reduce a child's problematic behaviors by developing and strengthening appropriate behaviors in their stead.

INDEX

motivational system 71, 72

N

natural consequences 11, 67, 72, 85, 88, 89, 91, 116, 176, 177, 181, 184, 202, 210
negative feedback cycle 66
neurologically impaired 34
neutralize 60, 101, 149

O

Oppositional Disorder 25
over-parenting 199

P

personal benefits XII
personal costs 106, 174
point system 71, 74, 188, 191
positive consequences 147, 207
positive feedback 198
praise 73, 196, 198-200
problematic behavior XI, XII, XIII, XV, 3, 15, 29, 31, 34, 35, 57, 62, 65, 67, 68, 78-81, 85, 91, 92, 93, 101, 117, 120, 132, 146, 170, 176, 189, 202, 204, 205, 212
punishment 7, 25, 53, 146, 147, 148, 179, 203, 212

R

reciprocal influence XI, 57, 83-85, 96, 131, 143, 200, 202
reinforcers 72-75
resilience 121, 122
respect 29, 37, 42, 51, 121, 140, 144, 163, 186, 217
responsibility III, XIV, 8, 10, 11, 34, 37, 53, 56, 61, 80, 82, 91, 153, 161-163, 186
rewards 13, 48, 49, 54, 71, 86, 108, 111, 114, 146, 147, 170, 194, 196, 197, 198

S

school XII, 2, 3, 9, 10-12, 18, 19, 20, 24, 28, 31, 32, 37, 41, 43, 44-46, 53, 56, 61
school Phobia 203
selective mutism 12

self-awareness 39
self-corrective consequences XIII, 206
self-corrective experiences 174, 175
self-esteem XV, 39, 43, 106, 127, 186, 199, 203, 207
self-management XIII, 182, 184, 185
self-oriented benefits 106
separation Anxiety 25, 203
short-term goals 194
signals 46, 139
skill deficit 189
skill development 146
social context 19, 65, 78, 128, 202, 204
social interaction 6, 27, 37
social reinforcers 73
social skills 27, 43, 44, 146, 163, 164
socialization 27, 163
spanking 5, 41
strategic parenting 120, 204
stress XI, 29, 32, 43, 62, 77, 103, 118, 127, 132, 162, 165, 181, 211
structure 15, 25, 43, 44, 137, 138
symbolic reinforcers 74

T

tantrums 78, 99
threats 40, 52, 86, 159
time-out 5, 25, 108, 138, 166, 167, 168, 169, 170, 171, 172, 173, 174
Transitioning 138
Tutorial Training 149, 150, 158, 159, 160

U

unintended consequences XIII, 8

V

verbal skills 20, 37, 108
verbal skills 37

W

warm fuzzies 174

SUGGESTED READINGS

Ayllon, T., and Azrin, N., *The Token Economy: A Motivational System for Therapy and Rehabilitation,* Prentice Hall, 1968.

Ayllon, T., Milan, M., Roberts, M., and McKee, J., *Correctional Rehabilitation and Management: A Psychological Approach,* Wiley Interscience, 1979.

Ayllon, T., and Freed, M., *Stopping Baby's Colic: The new program designed to relieve most infants' persistent crying in 3-7 days,* Putnam Publishing Group, 1989.

Ayllon, T., *How to Use Token Economy and Point Systems,* Pro-Ed, Inc., 1999 (2nd Ed.).

Hart, B., and Risley, T., *Meaningful Differences in the everyday experience of young American children,* Paul H. Brookes Publishing Co., Inc., 1995.

Jurkovic, G., *Lost Childhoods: The plight of the parentified child,* Brunner/Mazel, 1997.

Meichenbaum, D., *Cognitive-Behavior Modification,* Plenum Press, 1977.

Novak G., and Pelaez, M., *Child and Adolescent Development: A Behavioral Systems Approach,* Sage Publications Inc., 2004.

Seligman, M., Fall into Helplessness, *Psychology Today,* June, 1973.

ABOUT THE AUTHOR

William Byrd photography

Dr. Ted Ayllon is a clinical psychologist and Emeritus Professor of Psychology at Georgia State University, Fellow of the American Psychological Association, and a recipient of several awards including the 2007 Award for Distinguished Service to Behavior Analysis from the Society for the Advancement of Behavior Analysis. He has published over 80 scientific articles and several books on therapeutic methods involving the influence of the social environment on the development, maintenance, and elimination of emotional and behavioral problems of adults, teenagers, and children. Dr. Ayllon has a private practice in Atlanta, Georgia.

ABOUT ADI

Regardless of your industry or expertise, one thing remains constant: people power your business. At Aubrey Daniels International (ADI), we work closely with the world's leading organizations to accelerate their business performance by accelerating and sustaining the performance of the men and women whose efforts drive their success. We partner with our clients in a direct, practical, and sustainable way to get results faster and to increase organizational agility in today's unforgiving environment.

Founded in 1978, and headquartered in Atlanta, GA, we work with such diverse clients as Aflac, Duke Energy, Lafarge, Malt-O-Meal, M&T Bank, Medco, NASA, Roche Labs, Sears, and Tecnatom to systematically shape discretionary effort—where people consistently choose to do more than the minimum required. Our work with clients turns their strategy into action. We accomplish this not by adding new initiatives to their list, but by helping them make choices that are grounded in an ethical approach to people and business, by increasing effective and timely decision-making, and by establishing a culture of respect for each person's contribution, regardless of rank.

Whether at an individual, departmental, or organizational level, ADI provides tools and methodologies to help move people toward positive, results-driven accomplishments. ADI's products and services help anyone improve their business:

> **Assessments:** scalable, scientific analyses of systems, processes, structures, and practices, and their impact on individual and organizational performance

> **Coaching for Impact:** a behaviorally sound approach to coaching that maximizes individual contributions

> **Surveys:** a complete suite of proprietary surveys to collect

actionable feedback on individual and team performance, culture, safety, and other key drivers of business outcomes

Certification: ADI-endorsed mastery of client skills in the training, coaching, and implementation of our key products, processes, and/or technology

Seminars: a variety of engaging programs of practical tools and strategies for shaping individual and organizational success

Scorecards & Incentive Pay: an objective and results-focused alternative to traditional incentive pay systems

Sustaining Lean-Sigma Gains: a proactive and systematic process for managing safety that creates a culture of safe habits

Behavior-Based Safety: a proactive and systematic process for managing safety that creates a culture of safe habits

Safety Leadership: a behavioral approach to creating a high-performance safety culture through leadership action

Expert Consulting: custom, hands-on direction and support from seasoned behavioral science professionals in the design and execution of business-critical strategies and tactics

Speakers: accredited and celebrated thought leaders who can deliver the messages your organization needs on topics such as sustaining your gains, accelerating performance, and bringing out the best in others

aubreydaniels.com
aubreydanielsblog.com
facebook.com/Aubrey.Daniels.International
twitter.com/aubreydaniels
youtube.com/aubreydaniels

Performance Management Publications
Additional Resources

 Other People's Habits
Aubrey C. Daniels

 Bringing Out the Best in People
Aubrey C. Daniels

 Performance Management *(4th edition)*
Aubrey C. Daniels
James E. Daniels

 Oops! 13 Management Practices that Waste Time and Money
Aubrey C. Daniels

 Measure of a Leader
Aubrey C. Daniels
James E. Daniels

 A Good Day's Work
Alice Darnell Lattal
Ralph W. Clark

 Safe by Accident? Take the Luck out of Safety
Judy Agnew
Aubrey C. Daniels

 Removing Obstacles to Safety
Judy Agnew
Gail Snyder

 The Sin of Wages!
William B. Abernathy

 You Can't Apologize to a Dawg!
Tucker Childers

 Precision Selling
Joseph S. Laipple

 Human Incompetence
Thomas F. Gilbert

for more titles and information call
1.800.223.6191
or visit our web site
www.pmanagementpubs.com

REGISTER YOUR BOOK

Register your copy of *Head Strong* and receive exclusive reader benefits. Visit the Web site below and click on the "Register Your Book" link at the top of the page. Registration is free.

www.pmanagementpubs.com

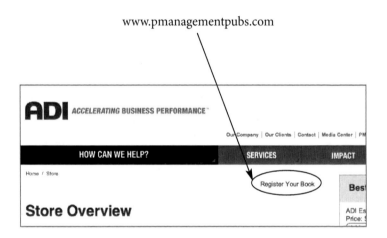